ENTREPRENI  NG

ENGAGING BUSINESS AND MISSION
FOR MARKETPLACE TRANSFORMATION

Entrepreneurial Church Planting

Engaging Business and Mission for Marketplace Transformation

Edited by

W. Jay Moon & Fredrick J. Long

GlossaHouse
Wilmore, KY
www.glossahouse.com

Digi-books

ENTREPRENEURIAL CHURCH PLANTING: ENGAGING BUSINESS AND MISSION FOR MARKETPLACE TRANSFORMATION

© GlossaHouse, LLC, and Digi-Books, 2018

GlossaHouse, LLC   and   Digi-books
110 Callis Circle   1067 N. Main St, # 229
Wilmore, KY 40309   Nicholasville, KY 40356
www.GlossaHouse.com   www.Digibooks.io
glossahouse@gmail.com   contact: roman@digibook.io

Entrepreneurial Church Planting: Engaging Business and Mission for Marketplace Transformation edited by W. Jay Moon & Fredrick J. Long. – Wilmore, KY : GlossaHouse; Nicholasville, KY : Digi-books, ©2018.

xii, 161 pages ; 22.86 cm. – (Digi-book series)

Contents: Introduction -- Introducing entrepreneurial church planting / W. Jay Moon -- Biblical foundations and theory -- Old Testament foundations: a vision for a holy missional community / Brian D. Russell -- The business behind and the work before Jesus / Fredrick J. Long – Jesus's entrepreneurial teaching and His earliest disciples / Fredrick J. Long -- Ecclesial entrepreneurs in Acts and Paul / Fredrick J. Long -- Great Commission: theological foundations and implications for marketplace ministry / Timothy C. Tennent -- Practices within the church -- Historical perspectives on entrepreneurial church planting / Samuel Lee -- Characteristics of entrepreneurial church planters / W. Jay Moon – Innovative fresh expressions of church / Winfield Bevins -- Starting points: robust missiology in the marketplace / W. Jay Moon

Includes bibliographical references and indexes.
ISBN 9781942697671 (paperback)
Library of Congress Control Number: 2018905952

1. Church development, New. 2. Entrepreneurship--Religious aspects--Christianity. 3. Business--Religious aspects--Christianity. I. Title. II. Moon, W. Jay. III. Long, Fredrick J., 1966-

BV652.25.E57 2018   277.97

Interior design by Fredrick J. Long; Cover design by T. Michael W. Halcomb

This book is dedicated to the creative and innovative church planters who are not content until the Great Commission is completed. You inspire and challenge the church to remain rooted in her tradition while expressing the Good News in various contexts such that it is always good and new.

DIGI-BOOK SERIES

SERIES EDITOR

W. Jay Moon

VOLUMES IN THE SERIES:

Volume 1: *Orality and Theological Training in the Twenty First Century*

Volume 2: *Social Entrepreneurship: Case Studies*

Volume 3: *Practical Evangelism for the Twenty First Century: Complexities and Opportunities*

Volume 4: *Intercultural Discipleship: Learning From Global Approaches to Spiritual Formation*

Volume 5: *Entrepreneurial Church Planting: Engaging Business and Mission for Marketplace Transformation*

Volume 6: *Missional Imagination* (forthcoming)

DIGI-BOOK SERIES

"I love to learn but I do not like to read," is a common statement heard among students in higher education. Digi-books provide learning resources for theological education that address the learning preferences of 21st century learners. Digi-books are based on the characteristics of contemporary digit-oral learners that prefer to: graze, dive, and connect. The Digi-book attracts digit-oral learners by providing introductory videos and embedded blogs in each chapter so that readers can graze over summaries of each chapter, dive into chapters of particular interest, and then connect with others asynchronously through embedded blog discussions. The end result is that contemporary learners create a learning community through the shared story in the Digi-book.

ACKNOWLEDGEMENTS

First of all, we would like to thank the Office of Faith, Work, and Economics (https://asburyseminary.edu/resources/ofwe/) at Asbury Theological Seminary for the grant to fund the development of this project. We would also like to thank the Digi-books team that envisioned and crafted the Digi-book series: Joshua Moon (media manager), Roman Randall (IT manager), and Pamela Moon (Executive Secretary). Each of these team members provides a valuable perspective and talent. In addition to gifting, they are each inspired by the Holy Spirit to provide Christ-honoring material as well as visionary innovation. It is truly a pleasure to work alongside this competent and godly team of servants. We also thank GlossaHouse for working so diligently to make this book available in print and Kindle. Their dedication to excellence in editing and cover design has made this project even more rewarding than it would have been otherwise.

"If you are an entrepreneur at heart with a passion for the Church and dream about planting a church that engages the two, *Entrepreneurial Church Planting* is written for you. You will discover you're not as strange as you thought or as alone as you may feel. The book offers biblical, theological, and historical examples of how the Church has engaged business and mission throughout history. It introduces the reader to contemporary models of marketplace churches and highlights skill sets needed for Entrepreneurial Church Planters. The book ends with practical processes to consider if you dare to live your dream."

—Dr. Larry W. Stoess, Church Planter, The United Methodist Church of the Promise, home of The Table Café, a pay-what-you-can community café in Louisville, Kentucky

"The American Church is facing unprecedented decline as our society rapidly changes. The good news is we're also seeing an unprecedented openness among established churches to start new forms of church that engage folks who are disinterested in Sunday morning services. Moon and Long offer a vital resource for churches and church planters seeking to start new forms of church in today's marketplace. Planters look differently than they did a decade ago and the skills needed for success are different. Moon and Long offer an excellent resource to sharpen these skills. As a leader of a network of fresh expressions and as a denominational leader helping others to start fresh expressions, I'm always looking for resources to guide my ministry and to pass along to church planters under my oversight. *Entrepreneurial Church Planting* will certainly be one of the books I give to practitioners needing practical ideas and theological support for their work. Entrepreneurial church planting can be a lonely and intimidating endeavor; so, books like this one help us practitioners feel affirmed in our callings and give us the resources we need for the journey."

—Rev. Luke Edwards, Pastor of King Street Church, Fresh Expressions Coordinator for the Western NC Conference UMC, Trainer and author for Fresh Expressions US (www.lukesedwards.com).

TABLE OF CONTENTS

PREFACE

The rise of the post-Christian context in the West has led retired Anglican Bishop Graham Cray in 2017 to conclude, "The long established ways of doing church are working less and less." Successive generations in the U.S. increasingly identify as post-Christian such that 48% of the Millennial generation is now considered to be post-Christian (Kinnaman, 2014). This has led Dr. Timothy C. Tennent to call the secularizing West one of the fastest growing mission fields.

At the same time, I regularly meet with church planters who are optimistic and enthusiastic about church planting for this generation. Many are launching or about to experiment with innovative approaches to plant churches that engage the marketplace. They are applying missional perspectives to reach this large mission field. This volume documents and explores these innovative approaches to church planting. The various authors describe how entrepreneurs are now finding where people are already gathering (or would gather) in the marketplace such that these businesses create a venue for a church. We are calling this Entrepreneurial Church Planting (ECP).

In order to encourage and explore further innovative ECP approaches, this volume provides both theoretical foundations and practical applications. It is arranged in three parts. Part I contains an introduction to the volume. Part II provides the biblical foundations to undergird ECP. Part III provides practical applications from both historical and contemporary examples and concludes with suggested starting points for experimentation and implementation. The goal is to encourage church planters to explore creative church planting approaches by engaging their faith in the marketplace. Asbury Theological Seminary is putting teeth into this effort by encouraging innovative church plants with partial sponsorship and training.

The best is yet to come. This is the vibe that arises from meeting with ECP planters that are now finding people coming to faith in venues where "church" was not normally discussed. I hope this volume stimulates further experimentation and discussion for the gospel to reach all sectors of society, including the marketplace.

PART I

INTRODUCTION

CHAPTER 1

Introducing Entrepreneurial Church Planting[1]

W. Jay Moon

Introduction

"Welcome to life on the fastest growing mission field in the world: North America," proclaimed Timothy C. Tennent, President of Asbury Theological Seminary, to incoming seminary students in 2016.[2] This proclamation recognizes that the church can no longer do "business as usual" as we move forward in the twenty-first century. While in previous generations the church was often considered to be a benevolent organization in the center of culture (like a chaplain of society), the Western church now finds herself marginalized and losing her public voice in the wider culture with decreasing church attendance in successive generations. Entrepreneurial church planters, however, are creatively entering this mission field by engaging and gathering communities of faith in the marketplace. These missional entrepreneurs leverage the networking and value creation provided by businesses in order to form communities of Christ followers among unchurched people. This chapter describes why entrepreneurial church planting is needed and provides guiding questions to direct these church planters to engage a new generation in the marketplace.

Post-Christian Reality

An objective observer of the church in North America would agree that the church is losing her overall influence in society. The question is, "How much influence is being lost and at what speed is this occurring?" David Kinnaman estimates 38% of people living in the continental U.S.

are actually "post-Christian" and "essentially secular in belief and practice," when adding the categories of "the unchurched, the never-churched and the skeptics" to those who report no religious affiliation.[3] An even more alarming trend is that "the younger the generation, the more post-Christian it is," as shown in Table 1 below:

- ❖ Millennials (born between 1984 and 2002) — 48%
- ❖ Gen X-ers (born between 1965 and 1983) — 40%
- ❖ Boomers (born between 1946 and 1964) — 35%
- ❖ Elders (born in 1945 or earlier) — 28%

Table 1—Percentage Post-Christian vs. Four Generations[4]

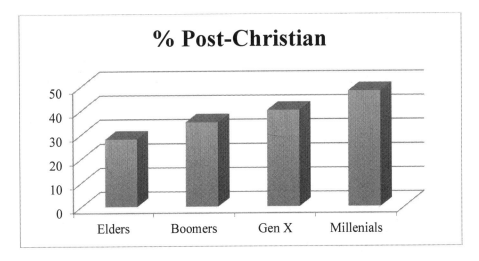

This trend is even more alarming when considering the plight of the Western European nations where church attendance has dropped to dismal levels. Is the fate of the church in North America destined to follow the secularization slide observed in the U.K.?

Guiding Questions

In the past, churches would often respond to decreasing church attendance by providing better preaching, better facilities, and more programs. While these have been good and needful interventions in the past, entrepreneurial church planters wrestle with a larger and more fundamental question,

1. "If large segments of the population (such as millennials) will not come to the existing churches, no matter how excellent the preaching, building, or programs, then what entrepreneurial approaches can be used to reach them?"

In other words, the church cannot assume that the post-Christian population will enter our traditional church buildings. As a result, we will need to consider creative venues outside the normal walls of the church buildings. In the past, perhaps churches have been planted in venues that are too limited in their ability to connect with people in their daily patterns of life and work, much like how the bonsai tree is limited in its growth.

A bonsai tree that was planted over 50 years ago will often have a thick trunk and knotted branches with a full display of leaves. Normally, families would enjoy having a picnic under the shade of a 50 year old tree. What is unique about the bonsai tree, however, is that the treetop only rises knee high. Standing at slightly over two feet high, the bonsai tree looks just like an ordinary tree except for its unusually small size.[5] What has limited the growth of this tree that would normally tower over a five-story building? Contrary to popular opinion, bonsai trees do not use genetically modified seeds to inhibit growth; rather, the small container is the culprit. The small container stifles the roots, thereby restricting tree growth to a fraction of its normal size.

Is it possible that church planters are planting churches in containers that are too restricted? It just may be perhaps that we are limiting the multiplication of churches by limiting the locations where they are planted; i.e., *churches are often planted in separate buildings that are disengaged from the daily patterns of life and work*. Especially since the industrial revolution, separate spaces have been designated for home, work, and worship. For someone to come worship at church then, they would have to intentionally leave work and home activities and enter a separate building once or twice a week. Is this restricted venue unintentionally stifling the (out)reach of the church?[6]

This leads to the second question that entrepreneurial church planters ask:

2. "Where are these unchurched people already gathering in the marketplace or what type of business ventures would draw them?"

Entrepreneurial church planters attempt to break out of restricted containers by planting churches in the marketplace as a means to engage those who are outside the church. For example, instead of asking millennials to leave their normal gathering locations such as coffee shops, cafes, pizza parlors, malls, movie theaters, etc., why not plant churches in these very venues? If these businesses do not exist, why not start a business that also serves as a venue for a church plant? Entrepreneurs recognize the capacity of business to develop networks through their value proposition. Church planters leverage this capacity in order to locate churches inside these businesses. (See the chapters on historical and contemporary examples.)

After considering the first two questions, the third question readily follows:

3. "How can entrepreneurs form communities of Christ followers in the marketplace through Christ honoring business ventures?"

Definition of Entrepreneurial Church Planting

With the above guiding questions as their marching orders, Entrepreneurial Church Planting (ECP) is defined as follows: *Entrepreneurial approaches to form communities of Christ followers among unchurched people through businesses in the marketplace.* ECP addresses the need to engage public society through the marketplace via entrepreneurial means. Such entrepreneurial church planters either start new businesses or work within existing businesses to plant churches in business venues. While many traditional church planters were reluctant to combine entrepreneurship and church planting, entrepreneurial church planters are eager to combine the two in order to realize the synergy gained by joining forces.[7]

The marketplace is used as a broad term to describe the network of relationships whereby people exchange value with one another. Businesses often have a network of relationships that form as a result of their supply chains and their distribution networks. Instead of regarding these networks as simply secular venues, entrepreneurial church planters regard these relationships as fertile soil for church planting. This is not necessarily easy work, but it is missional and vital from the perspective of the *missio Dei*. The need for ECP, then, is rooted directly in the mission of God to redeem humanity. Although this book describes several contemporary examples, the necessity and practice of ECP is firmly rooted in biblical soil.

The Biblical Soil for ECP

In contemporary North American culture, the traditional church has found it challenging to penetrate the marketplace. Michael Moynagh notes, "It is not easy for the church to form Christian lives in work, volunteering and leisure when the formation takes place some distance away. The teaching of practices at church may have a level of generality that fails to engage with the specifics of a person's life."[8] Yet, there are biblical examples of church plants amidst this network of relationships (where people spend the majority of their waking moments) called the marketplace. While a biblical/theological basis for ECP is discussed further in chapters 2-6, this chapter will here briefly summarize Paul's entrepreneurial church planting.

The Apostle Paul, church planter extraordinaire, worked alongside Priscilla and Aquila as a tentmaker in Corinth, the political and economic center of Greece and the "transit point for all maritime trade between Rome and the prosperous Roman province of Asia."[9] Although the details of this tent-making business venue are not clear, New Testament scholar Craig S. Keener notes, "multistory apartment buildings with ground-floor workshops were common; a number of urban artisans lived onsite, sometimes in a mezzanine level above their ground-floor shops … many sold from shops in their homes."[10] Keener then concludes that Priscilla and Aquila may have lived on the floor above their artisan shop. Since the trade guilds were strong in Paul's day, he had access to the tent-making guild and the network of relationships connected to their business. It seems that Paul intentionally worked in the marketplace in order to have access to business networks for church planting.

While this business aspect of the Apostle Paul is often cited to support the Business As Mission movement, what is less discussed is the church plant that resulted from this business activity. In Romans 16:3–5 and 1 Corinthians 16:19, we discover that a church met at Priscilla and Aquila's home, which was likely connected to their business, thereby making this a potent example of ECP. Paul praised Priscilla and Aquila when he noted, "They risked their lives for me. Not only I but all the churches of the Gentiles are grateful for them" (Romans 16:4). Certainly, these entrepreneurial church planters were significant in Paul's mind.

This was not an isolated incident for Paul, however. When Paul traveled earlier to Philippi, Lydia, a "dealer in purple cloth" (Acts 16:14) responded to Paul's message such that Lydia and her whole household were baptized. Lydia, then invited Paul and his companions to her home (Acts 16:15). If we consider again that her home and business place were likely connected, then Paul was actually visiting her business venue for an extended time of teaching and ministry. Paul again meets this gathering of believers at Lydia's home/business in order to encourage them prior to travelling on to Thessalonica (Acts 16:40). It may be that Paul "stumbled" upon this ECP approach in Lydia's business such that he later intentionally used this approach in Priscilla and Aquila's business.

Although traditional church planters may be reluctant to engage the marketplace, Jesus did not seem to have the same reticence. In fact, he overwhelmingly engaged topics related to the marketplace, and he often visited the marketplace. In addition, most of the divine interventions in the Book of Acts appeared in the marketplace. This is depicted in Figure 1 below.[11]

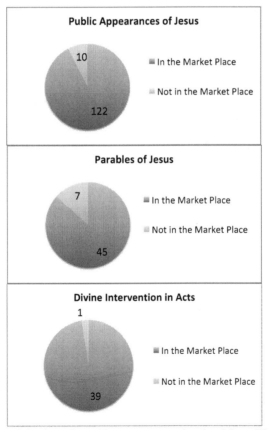

Figure 1—Marketplace Engagement in the New Testament

Far from being a side issue, Greg Forster notes that the Bible places a great deal of importance on issues and concerns in the marketplace,

> [T]he Bible speaks at length about work and economics. Our daily labor is the subject of extensive scriptural concern; passages running from Genesis 1 through Revelation 22 teach us to view our work as central to the meaning of our lives. We are taught to view our work as service to God and neighbor, to work diligently in an honest calling, and to persevere under the challenges of a fallen and broken world.[12]

The Bible regularly and often speaks about the centrality of work in our lives, yet this is not often the topic of conversation from pulpits across North America. This reality led Mark Greene to conclude, "The 98 percent of Christians who are not in church-paid work are, on the whole, not equipped or envisioned for mission ... in 95 percent of their waking lives. What a tragic waste of human potential!"[13] What would it look like if "normal" Christians were to consider that it is God's plan for them to carry out their missional calling WITHIN the marketplace and not in spite of it? How could they utilize their gifting, networks, resources, etc. in mission with God through the marketplace to reach unchurched people? Instead of assigning church planting solely to paid clergy, what if those skilled in entrepreneurship were awakened to utilize their talents for business and calling in mission as church planters within the marketplace? Fortunately, we have historical examples, grounded in missiological roots that have done exactly this.

Historical Examples with Missiological Roots

Lesslie Newbigin and the ensuing missional church movement have pleaded for churches to regain their missional calling by finding their role in the *Missio Dei*. Newbigin states strongly, "A Christian community which makes it own self enlargement its primary task may be acting against God's will."[14] He then implores the church to ...

> Go into every sector of public life to claim it for Christ, to unmask the illusions which have remained hidden and to expose all areas of public life to the illumination of the gospel. But that will only happen as and when local congregations renounce an

introverted concern for their own life, and recognize that they exist for the sake of those who are not members, as sign, instrument, and foretaste of God's redeeming grace for the whole life of society.[15]

Entrepreneurial church planters heed Newbigin's call to engage public life by utilizing their entrepreneurial capacities in the economic sector. The resulting businesses and faithful communities of Christ followers are to be a sign, instrument, and foretaste of the kingdom of God for the sake of those outside the walls of the existing church.

Dallas Willard recognized the tremendous potential of engaging the business world as he noted,

> What far too few either recognize or appreciate today are the opportunities available for spreading God's goodness, grace, and provision far and wide through the systems and distribution networks that exist as a direct result of industrial and commercial organizations and their professionals. Therefore the "business world" is a critical aspect that cannot be overlooked and must be fully appreciated as vital in God's plan to overcome evil with good.[16]

While not being naïve about the potential for abuse in business, Willard further described the tremendous kingdom potential through business that is done with integrity, honesty, and transparency,

> [L]ocal business people may be farther ahead in the ways of the kingdom than those leading a local church. Business is an amazingly effective means of delivering God's love to the world by loving, serving, and providing for one another. God loves the world (John 3:16), and because he does, he has arranged the enterprise and organization of business as a primary moving force to demonstrate this love throughout human history. Thus, the field of business and its unique knowledge fall perfectly into what can and should be understood as an essential realm of human activity that can and must come under the influence and control of God's benevolent reign.[17]

To neglect the marketplace then is to neglect the reach of the *missio Dei* in a vital sector of society.

Twenty-First Century Circuit Riders?

Chapter 7 provides historical examples of entrepreneurs that have successfully engaged in mission, resulting in church planting beginning with the early church to the present time. A few brief sketches of the Wesleyan movement should suffice here to demonstrate that the ECP approach has a trustworthy track record.

In eighteenth-century England, John Wesley realized that there were large groups of people that were not coming to the church. (This should sound familiar to contemporary readers living in Western contexts.) Instead of waiting for them to come to the church, he realized that he needed to go where they were already gathering. He visited the market places, brick yards, coal mines, etc. in order to bring the gospel to those who were unchurched instead of asking them to clean up and come into the church. Tennent describes this in some detail:

> His [John Wesley's] favorite venue for preaching was graveyards and market places…. Markets were good because there was often a cross at the market. In 18th century England it was not unusual for a cross to be placed in the trading markets as a sign to remind people of the importance of honesty in public trade. So, Wesley could be outside in a very public place, and yet preach under a cross… Wesley's famous line, "All the world is my parish" is rooted in these new realities: Closed pulpits and their decision to move beyond formal parish lines to embrace a rather bold ecclesiology.[18]

Although hesitant at first, Wesley observed that this practice resulted in a movement, gathering communities of Christ followers among unchurched people in the marketplace. Wesley's own business (yes, he was an ardent businessman and theologian!) earned a profit that is estimated at 4 to 5 million dollars in today's currency.[19] He realized the great good that this business profit could provide in his sermon on "The Use of Money":[20]

> In the hands of his children, it [money] is food for the hungry, drink for the thirsty, raiment for the naked: It gives to the traveller and the stranger where to lay his head. By it we may supply the place of an husband to the widow, and of a father to the fatherless. We may be a defence for the oppressed, a means of

health to the sick, of ease to them that are in pain; it may be as eyes to the blind, as feet to the lame; yea, a lifter up from the gates of death![21]

Reflecting on the missional significance of business and money in the marketplace, Wesley concluded in the same sermon, "It is therefore of the highest concern that all who fear God know how to employ this valuable talent; that they be instructed how it may answer these glorious ends, and in the highest degree."[22] Entrepreneurial church planters are living out their entrepreneurial gifting and missional calling in the marketplace, as Wesley suggested.

The spark generated by Wesley's entrepreneurial approach eventually spread like a wildfire on the American frontier as Methodist circuit riders traveled to locations where pioneers lived and worked. Instead of waiting for pioneers to come to the existing churches, circuit riders preached at local gathering spots to form communities of Christ followers. Kenneth Kinghorn describes this activity:

> Eighteenth-century conference minutes listed the preaching places precisely. Sites included taverns, cabins, stores, poorhouses, forts, barns, woodland clearings and riverboats. On one occasion, a circuit rider preached in a gambling house. A layperson said, "In Jesus' time some made the house of God a den of thieves, but now the Methodists have changed a den of thieves into a house of God…. By the mid 1800s, American Methodism had become by far the largest and most spiritually influential religious body in the nation.[23]

The parallels between the eighteenth-century Methodist circuit riders and twenty-first century entrepreneurial church planters are compelling. Both saw their missional calling and were willing to engage the locations where people outside the existing church were gathering. Both were pioneers, willing to take risks in the marketplace so that the church could fulfill her role as a sign, foretaste, and instrument of the kingdom of God[24]. Both recognized the potential of entrepreneurial experiments and decided to employ their talents for the kingdom of God. Is it possible that entrepreneurial church planters are the twenty-first century equivalent of the eighteenth-century Methodist circuit riders with the potential to once again transform the spiritual landscape of North America?

Conclusion

Due to the missional context that the North American church now finds herself in, entrepreneurial church planters are engaging the marketplace as a mission field. After serving the Anglican Church in the UK for many years, retired Bishop Graham Cray concluded, "The long established ways of doing church are working less and less."[25] As a result, he was instrumental in forming the Fresh Expressions movement in the UK,[26] which has spread to the U.S. and other areas.[27] He recognized that innovative approaches for church planting, including those in the marketplace, are needed to stem the decline of the church's influence in the Western world.

This chapter recommends that church planters consider the potential of the marketplace to create large networks based upon authentic relationships through mutual exchange. I am not suggesting, however, that the churches should be operated as businesses; rather, businesses can be operated with a focus on church planting. Entrepreneurial church plants must have a double bottom line: missional purpose AND entrepreneurial viability. One without the other is not sufficient. If there is not a missional purpose, then entrepreneurial church plants can devolve into a business that does not seek to worship God (like Jesus condemned in John 2 when he cleansed the temple). If entrepreneurial church plants are not financially viable, then they will not survive to create long-term impact. By focusing on both missional purpose and entrepreneurial viability, entrepreneurial church plants may open new possibilities for church planters. Some of these possibilities include the following:

1. <u>Teams</u>: Unlike the common myth of a lone entrepreneur working silently in their garage, most entrepreneurs require a team. Cooney noted, "It is arguable that despite the romantic notion of the entrepreneur as a lone hero, the reality is that successful entrepreneurs either built teams about them or were part of a team throughout."[28] Entrepreneurial church plants have the potential to energize and engage laity in the church who did not see their vital role in the kingdom beforehand. For example, Chris Sorenson, planter of an Anglican church inside a café called the Camp House, confided in me, "If I had to do this church plant all over again, the first person that I would hire would be an accountant!" How many accountants in the church presently see their vital role in using their skills in the mission of God? Entrepreneurial church plants can energize the 'secular professionals' in the church so that they now have a vital role in

Lauren Lyons

the church planting movement.[29]

2. Ecclesiology: While great gains in theology have been gained throughout the history of the church, her very survival has required cultural adaptation.[30] If the cultural straight jackets are laid aside and new innovations are explored for the shaping of the church, then new possibilities for the flourishing of the church can be realized. In short, the bonsai plant can break free from the small containers that limit growth and the same seed can be planted among less restricted locations for wider reach. While care has to be taken to ensure the church's fidelity to her identity, the mission of the church requires a deep engagement with the surrounding culture, including the vast network of relationships called the marketplace. New ecclesial forms will likely result from this type of creative and entrepreneurial thinking.

3. Lay/Bi-vocational Ministry: While the employment of full time pastors will not likely come to an end any time soon, entrepreneurial church plants consider the value of pastors remaining connected to their own circles of exchange in the marketplace, following the example of Paul in Corinth. For example, an entrepreneurial church plant that started as a result of a tech startup found that the business addressed some of the most pressing needs for jobs in the city. As a result, the pastors did not want to leave their work for full-time pastoring; otherwise, this would remove them from the very context to influence the surrounding culture.[31] At the very least, entrepreneurial church plants allow church planters and their stakeholders to explore various questions and options for the employment and compensation of church planters.

To guide further reflection, discussion, and praxis, the following chapters will discuss a biblical and theological basis for ECP, to be followed by historical and then contemporary examples. I will also present a paradigm for the type of church planters that are ideally suited for this expression of the church. Our hope is that this type of probing will lead to further experimentation and innovation by entrepreneurial church planters worldwide.

To explore this missional innovation in the marketplace, we will start where the Bible starts—in Genesis. This biblical foundation will be the topic of the next chapter.

---

[1] Portions of the material for this chapter were originally published in W. Jay Moon, "Entrepreneurial Church Planting." *Great Commission Research Journal* 9.1 (2017): 56–70.

[2] Timothy C. Tennent, "Homiletical Theology" (Opening Convocation Address, Asbury Theological Seminary, September 2016), http://timothytennent.com/2016/09/13/my-2016-opening-convocation-address-homiletical-theology/.

[3] Cathy Lynn Grossman, "Secularism Grows as More U.S. Christians Turn 'churchless,'" *Religion News Service*, October 24, 2014, http://religionnews.com/2014/10/24/secularism-is-on-the-rise-as-more-u-s-christians-turn-churchless/.

[4] Ibid.

[5] For a colorful portrayal of the beauty of bonsai trees, see http://www.bonsaiempire.com/blog/bonsai-movie

[6] A similar argument is made in: Ken Hemphill and Kenneth Priest, *Bonsai Theory of Church Growth*, Revised and Expanded ed. (Tigerville, SC: Auxano, 2011).

[7] The author still affirms the value and need for traditional approaches to church planting. This as a "both/and" instead of an "either/or" in order to reach various groups of people.

[8] Michael Moynagh and Philip Harrold, *Church for Every Context: An Introduction to Theology and Practice* (London: SCM, 2012), 3885–6 Kindle.

[9] Craig S. Keener, *The IVP Bible Background Commentary: New Testament*, 2nd ed. (Downers Grove, IL: InterVarsity Press, 2014), 379.

[10] Ibid.

[11] R. Paul Stevens, *Work Matters: Lessons from Scripture* (Grand Rapids: Eerdmans, 2012), 135.

[12] Greg Forster, "Introduction: What Are People Made For?," in *The Pastor's Guide to Fruitful Work and Economic Wisdom*, ed. Greg Forster and Drew Cleveland (Grand Rapids: Made to Flourish, 2012), 9.

[13] Ibid., 6.

[14] Lesslie Newbigin, *The Gospel in a Pluralist Society* (Grand Rapids: Eerdmans, 1989), 135.

[14] Ibid., 233.

[15] Ibid., 233.

[16] Dallas Willard and Gary Black Jr., *The Divine Conspiracy Continued: Fulfilling God's Kingdom on Earth* (New York: Harper One, 2014), 201.

[17] Ibid., 203.

[18] Timothy C. Tennent, "Homiletical Theology" (Opening Convocation Address, Asbury Theological Seminary, September 2016), http://timothytennent.com/2016/09/13/my-2016-opening-convocation-address-homiletical-theology/.

[19] David Wright, *How God Makes the World A Better Place: A Wesleyan Primer on Faith, Work, and Economic Transformation* (Grand Rapids: Christian's Library Press, 2012).

[20] As a businessman and theologian, Wesley was not naïve about the potential harm of wealth, as noted in other sermons (e.g., The dangers of riches). This is instructive for contemporary contexts. Wesley saw the good and bad, yet was willing to explore this potential for kingdom benefit. Theologians that I have talked with that have personally owned their own business often have a very different perspective on profit, markets, and the general potential for businesses to create flourishing societies than those who have not owned a business.

[21] Wesley's sermons are available at http://wesley.nnu.edu/john-wesley/the-sermons-of-john-wesley-1872-edition/the-sermons-of-john-wesley-theological-topic/. Several of his sermons dealt with topics related to money, including:
- Sermon 87 - The Danger of Riches 1 Tim 6:9
- Sermon 112 - The Rich Man and Lazarus Luke 16:31
- Sermon 50 - The Use of Money Luke 16:9
- Sermon 51 - The Good Steward Luke 21:2
- Sermon 108 - On Riches Matt 19:24
- Sermon 126 - On the Danger of Increasing Riches Ps 62:10

[22] Ibid.

[23] Kenneth Cain Kinghorn, "Offer Them Christ with Bibles in Hand & God's Spirit in their Hears, the Early Circuit Riders," *The Asbury Herald* 117.1 (2007): 13.

[24] Leslie Newbigin, *The Gospel in a Pluralist Society* (Grand Rapids: Eerdmans), 1989

[25] Personal conversation with the author and Graham Cray in York, England in January, 2017.

[26] ECP is a subset of Fresh Expressions since not every Fresh Expression is engaged in the marketplace, though some are.

[27] For example, Sang Rak Joo's forthcoming dissertation research at Asbury Theological Seminary documents the increased social capital resulting from recent ECPs in South Korea.

[28] Thomas M. Cooney, "Editorial: What Is an Entrepreneurial Team?," *International Small Business Journal* 23.3 (2005): 226.

[29] Consider the vital fields that businesses engage that can now be energized to fulfill their missional calling, such as finance, accounting, management, marketing, to name a few.

[30] A. F. Walls, *The Missionary Movement in Christian History: Studies in the Transmission of Faith* (Maryknoll, NY: Orbis, 1996).

[31] A forthcoming PhD dissertation by Samuel Lee at Asbury Theological Seminary documents this ECP. For a partial description, see: Samuel Lee, "Can We Measure the Success and Effectiveness of Entrepreneurial Church Planting?," *Evangelical Review of Theology* 40.4 (2016): 327–45.

PART II

BIBLICAL FOUNDATIONS

CHAPTER 2

Old Testament Foundations:
A Vision for a Holy Missional Community

Brian D. Russell

"Business was originated to produce happiness, not to pile up millions."

—B. C. Forbes

Introduction

The Scriptures of ancient Israel cast a bold vision of God's calling of a holy worshipping community that exists as a means of blessing the nations. In the twenty-first century, God's people are sensing an emerging opportunity to spread the Gospel by engaging 'not yet' Christ followers in the market place through entrepreneurial church planting (ECP). This essay will explore the foundations provided by the Old Testament for guiding the practice of ECP. The following discussion aims to offer a heuristic framework for church planters aiming to influence and witness in and to the marketplace. God's vision for God's Old Testament people was to live as a missional community that reflected God's character to the nations, among the nations, and for the nations. Given its brevity, this essay will focus principally on Israel's foundational story in Genesis–Deuteronomy with limited reference to the rest of the Old Testament canon.

Vocation and Mission for God's People in the Old Testament

ECP assumes a context in which a church planter is actively engaged in the marketplace. In today's language we often use the word "bivocational" to capture this dynamic balance between ministry and employment in the marketplace. This model stands mostly outside of the aims and content of the Old Testament. In the Old Testament, God calls a people to himself and establishes them *in the land of Canaan* to be a "light to the nations" (Isa 42:6; 49:6) rather than as a missionary movement *to the nations*. Thus, most Old Testament institutions assume a sedentary people living as a nation in the midst of nations that do not yet know God. There were no formal attempts to evangelize the other nations by going to live and work among them. The prophet Jonah who travelled to Nineveh is the principal exception that proves the rule.

Of course, Israel's ancestors (Abraham, Isaac, Jacob and their families) lived out God's mission as semi-nomadic herdsmen to be agents of blessing (Gen 12:3b). They bore witness to the peoples around them while their life in Canaan foreshadowed the New Testament mission of bearing the Gospel to the ends of the earth (Matt 28:16–20; Acts 1:8). These herdsmen provide the closest examples of the lifestyle of a modern entrepreneurial church planter. Abraham, Isaac, Jacob, and their families moved into region of Canaan and lived among the population as newcomers. However, after the settlement of God's people in the land, Israel functioned more as a political entity under polity of the Torah. Israel lived out its life as a "light to the nations" through the proscribed institutions of prophet, priest, and king.[1] These "offices," particularly priest and king, were permanent positions with support from Israel as a whole. The tribe of Levi whose members received a tithe for their material support taught the law and performed cultic functions in Israel.[2]

The closest Old Testament analogy for ECP once Israel entered the land after the deliverance from Egypt would be the prophets who were drawn from various spheres of Israelite society and received support through avenues not necessarily related to their role as a prophet. Most famously, Amos defended himself against the charge of prophesying for money by declaring, "I'm no prophet nor a son of a prophet, but I am a herdsman and a dresser of sycamore trees" (Amos 7:14).[3] In other words, he was not a religious professional who earned a living through prophecy. As we'll see below, the Old Testament's contribution to the ECP movement is less about examples and models than it is about providing a theological and ethical foundation for embodying a robust missional community.

The Old Testament and the Mission of God

The overarching biblical narrative moves from Creation to Fall to the formation of Israel: God's New Humanity to Jesus the Messiah to the Church and finally to New Creation. God's mission is the central theme of the Bible's story.[4] The Old Testament is critical for understanding the first half of the Bible's missional drama.

Creation and Fall

The Old Testament opens with narratives that offer the background to the story of God's calling of Israel to serve as a missional community for the sake of all humanity. Genesis 1:1–2:25 narrates the story of God's creation of an abundant world. In this world, humanity existed as the climax of God's creative work (1:26–31). Created in the image of God, men and women lived as visible reflections of the invisible Creator.[5] Humanity was to fill the earth and provide leadership for it on behalf of the Creator (1:28, 2:15). These chapters offer a glimpse of life as God intended. [Do you think it may be worthwhile to point out that God provided work BEFORE the fall in order to dignify humanity and participate in this co-creation?] There was relational wholeness between humanity and God. There was mutuality between men and women. There was harmony between humanity and the earth. Work as God intended was purposeful and integral to God's creational designs. God worked to move creation from a chaotic beginning (Gen 1:2) to "good" on Days 1–5 (Gen 1:4, 1:10, 1:12, 1:18, and 1:21) to "very good" on Day 6 (Gen 1:31).
        Humanity also had a vocation. Humanity originally served as a holy community with a mission. The mission was to serve as God's agents to care for the creation and witness to creation's invisible Creator. Genesis 1–2 focuses on the creation of men and women to emphasize the communal nature of life. To be human is to be part of a community and to work within that community. Humanity's original work involved serving as stewards of creation and filling the earth (Gen 1:26–31). In Gen 2:15, God places humanity in the garden "to serve

and to take care of it." The nuance here suggests meaningful and purposeful work and engagement with creation. The command to "fill the earth" (Gen 1:28) involves humanity's mission to cover the earth with persons created in God's image as a means of witnessing to the rest of creation about the Creator God.

The language of holiness is not explicit in Gen 1–2, but the implied ethic for humanity is a faithful service in dedication to God's aims. The giving of the prohibition against eating from the tree of the knowledge of good and evil serves as the boundary marker between obedience and disobedience (2:16–17; cf. 2:9).

Genesis 3:1–11:25 offers a series of narratives and genealogies that explain how the perfect world that God created shifted to the broken and lost world in which we live today. There is alienation between God and humanity, desire for domination between humans, and a more tenuous relationship between humanity and the environment. In the New Testament, Paul summarizes the plight of humanity and creation itself in the book of Romans: "For all have sinned and fall short of the glory of God" (3:23 ESV) and "For the creation was subjected to futility, not willingly, but because of him who subjected it, in hope that the creation itself will be set free from its bondage to corruption and obtain the freedom of the glory of the children of God" (8:20–21 ESV). These realities find their roots in Genesis 3–11. The narratives of Adam, Eve, and the serpent (3:1–24); Abel, Cain, and Seth (4:1–26); Noah and the great flood (Gen 6–9) and the tower of Babel (11:1–9) describe the spread and infestation of sin into all humanity and its institutions as well as the brokenness of creation itself. These chapters also highlight the grace of God in his dealings with his lost creation. The genealogies record multiplication of humanity and its filling of the earth (Gen 5; 10; 11:10–25).

After Babel, humanity is now spread out across the planet as God intended (11:8–9; cf. 1:28 and 9:1). The irony of the post-Babel world is that humanity has now filled the earth as God desired, but it is a lost humanity rather than one living as a holy, missional people. Thus, the missional need is great. Here, the mission of God becomes the salvation of a lost humanity and the restoration of a broken world. This is the mission to which God calls us to participate as entrepreneurial church planters. Genesis 1–11 also describes the world in which entrepreneurial church planters will operate. It is no longer the perfect world that God intended (Gen 1–2). Church planters carry good news to a broken world and lost humanity (Gen 3–11) in anticipation of full restoration and abundance in the New Creation.

Israel: God's New Humanity (Israel's Ancestors)

Agents of Blessing. God's mission of salvation will reach its pinnacle in the life, death, and resurrection of Jesus. Post-Resurrection, Jesus will send forth the church in the power of the Spirit into the nations (Act 1:8) to make disciples (Matt 28:18–20). But this mission begins with a calling forth of a new humanity out of the old world to become agents of blessing for the nation. God calls Abram and Sarah (Gen 11:27–12:9). Genesis 12–50 narrates God's dealings with Israel's ancestors. There are critical lessons for ECP.

Blessed to be a Blessing. God's missional calling of Abram and his family is paradigmatic for understanding the call to ECP. In Gen 12:1–9, God sends Abram and his family to a new land. Gen 12:3b is critical for understanding the Old Testament's witness to God's mission: "all peoples on earth will be blessed through you."[6] The calling of Abram is a missional calling for the sake of all peoples. Notice the canonical setting of Abram's call. It follows immediately the stories of Creation and Fall in Gen 1–11. Who are the peoples whom God will bless through Abram? None other than the peoples and nations described in the opening chapters of the Bible (Gen 1–11 esp. the Table of Nations [10:1–32]). In other words, God calls a *particular* people for the sake of a *universal* mission. Church planter Alex McManus puts it this way: "The Gospel comes to us on its way to someone else. The Gospel comes to us on its way to someplace else."[7]

Worship. The stories of Israel's ancestors testify to the power of worship for staying grounded as an itinerant people. As Abraham, Isaac, and Jacob sojourned in new lands, they consistently worshipped the Lord by building altars (Abraham: 12:7; 13:4, 18; 22:9; cf. 21:33; Isaac: 26:25 and Jacob: 33:20 and 35:1–7). They memorialized significant events and times in their missional living in new places with worship. This serves as a signal to entrepreneurial church planters to ground missional activities in an ongoing pattern of worship and celebration.

God's Faithfulness to God's Promises. Genesis 12–50 serves as prelude to the Torah's two preeminent acts of salvation: Exodus and Sinai. The emphasis of Genesis 12–50 is the establishment by God's faithfulness of a new humanity that will serve as agents of blessing.

Moving out of the colossal failings of Genesis 1–11, Genesis 12–50 demonstrates a dynamic interplay between God's grace and human response, but the emphasis is on how God drives the actions forward by grace and faithfulness. When we read the stories of Abraham/Sarah, Isaac/Rebekah, Jacob, Esau, and their families, we find a series of missteps and family tensions in their stories. They may be the heroes and heroines, but they are broken and lost apart from God. When reading Genesis 12–50, there are high points of human faithfulness. For example, Abram goes in response to God's calling (Gen 12:4). Abram responds with faith to God's promises (Gen 15:6). Jacob holds onto to God for a blessing (Gen 32:22–32). Joseph (Gen 39) acts justly in difficult circumstances. But just as often there are failings: Abram lies about his relationship to Sarah (Gen 12:10–20). Abram and Sarah act independently of God's intention by using Sarah's servant Hagar as a surrogate (Gen 16). Jacob schemes his brother Esau out of his birthright and blessing (Gen 27–28). Joseph acts arrogantly with his brothers who in turn sell him into slavery (Gen 37).

Yet in the midst of this brokenness, God advance God's mission. God does this by consistently subverting the typical channels of human power. These actions highlight God's faithfulness and demonstrate that the Gospel's ultimate success depends on God's power and grace apart from human ingenuity and giftedness. First, God sends God's people to a new land–Canaan. Canaan was inhabited during this time but for most of Near Eastern history the power centers were Mesopotamia and Egypt. God called Abram out of Mesopotamia. Abram's family roots were in Ur (Gen 11:31). Second, throughout Genesis, God consistently prefers to bypass the firstborn son to work with a younger sibling. The first occurrence was with God's favoring of Abel's sacrifice over Cain's (Gen 4:1–16). As Abram's family grew, this phenomenon occurred in each generation– Isaac over Ishmael, Jacob over Esau, and Joseph over his 10 older brothers. In the ancient world (and in some modern cultures), the firstborn son received preferential treatment and inherited the majority of the father's estate as a means of a family leveraging its resources. By utilizing younger siblings, God demonstrates that the Gospel moves forward apart from human attempts to shape the future. Last, throughout Genesis 12–50, God's people experience the challenge of childlessness. Abraham/Sarah, Isaac/Rebekah, and Jacob/Rachel go through significant periods of time as childless couples. This is significant because God had promised Abraham descendants as numerous as the stars in the sky and sands on the seashore (Gen 22:17 cf. 15:5). In each case, God blesses these couples with a child who will be significant in the advancement of God's mission. In tandem with the previous element of the bypassing of the firstborn, God shows that the future depends on God's promises rather than on human best practices. This lesson is critical for ECP and invites a radical openness to a future that advances by God's blessings beyond our trust in business plans and church planting best practices alone. It also illustrates that God can work despite our failings and our brokenness. During difficult days in ministry and work, remembering this reality can be deeply comforting.

Amen

Israel: God's New Humanity (Exodus)

Exodus 19:4–6 captures the Old Testament's vision for God's people. God's people will serve as a "kingdom of priests and a holy nation" for the rest of the world.[8] These phrases summarize the vocation for God's people in the world today. They combine a vision for a holy people that exists to reflect and testify to God's character in the world, to the world, and for the world.

Created by Grace. Grace is the basis for the relationship between God and God's missional people. At Sinai, before offering covenant, God grounds the relationship between himself and Israel by *rehearsing* the past: "You have seen what I did to Egypt, how I carried you on eagle's wings and brought you to myself" (Exod 19:4). These are the opening words of God on Sinai. Israel's exists free from Egyptian oppression because God acted on their behalf. God's actions as the creator of the *relationship* between God and God's people is restated memorably at the beginning of the Ten Commandments: "I am the LORD your God who brought you out of Egypt out of the house of slavery" (Exod 20:2).[9]

Egypt is now past history. The deliverance from Egypt serves as the definitive marker of God's people's movement from death to life, from oppression that stifled mission to liberation for God's mission. Israel celebrated Passover (Exod 12:1–13:16) as a means of remembering God's grace in their lives and inculcating this reality across the generations of God's people. Like the models of Israel's ancestors who build altars, the remembrance of God's saving actions must be part of the culture of ECP.

Eucharist

Egypt serves as a warning for God's people. Post-deliverance Egypt's function in the Torah is to serve as a negative example for Israel to avoid. The poor treatment of Israel by the Egyptians is used to remind God's people to avoid replicating the injustices of Egypt onto others (Exod 22:21; 23:9; Lev 18:3; 19:34, 36). The message is clear: *A redeemed and liberated people must live out their new lives in distinctively different ways than their former oppressors.* This is the heart of the relational implications of holiness.

Response to Grace. Our identity as God's missional people is a lifestyle consciously lived in response to God's grace. In the Old Testament, God's identity shaping/future altering actions in the Exodus and victory at the Red Sea serve as the basis for Israel's life as a missional nation for the sake of the world. The goal of the liberation of God's people from Egypt and the forging of a covenant is a vibrant relationship between God and Israel through which God's people are sanctified for service in God's mission.

The necessity of sanctification is critical for a missional theology. If as God's people, we do not live out holy lives before a watching world, we may ultimately testify to a different God. ECP faces the same risks as Israel. In the Old Testament, Israel was the sole representative of God among the nations. As the entrepreneurial church planters engage increasingly secularized people as well as practitioners of alternative spiritualities in workplaces, it is critical for God's people to reflect God's character and heart in interactions with others.

The warning of the Old Testament is this: *It was easier for God to get Israel out of Egypt than it was for God to remove Egypt from Israel.* This is less an indicator of the limitations of God's power than it is a recognition of human intransigence. Israel is often described as stubborn or "stiff necked" (Exod 32:9; 33:3, 5; 34:9; Deut 9:6, 13; 10:16; 31:27; 2 Kgs 17:14; Neh 9:16–17; Jer 17:23). Israel's refusal and seeming inability to live faithfully as God's people muted Israel's testimony to the nations and serves as a witness to ECP of the sky-high stakes of unfaithfulness and disobedience.

What does it look like to live for the Lord today? How does the Old Testament envision a life of missional holiness? Exodus 19:5–6 invites God's people at Sinai to "truly listen to God's voice and keep God's covenant." The response to grace is faithful obedience. By embracing faithfulness, God's people gain a new identity as "God's treasured possession" out of all nations. The entire earth belongs to the

Lord so Israel as God's treasured possession serves vocationally as a "kingdom of priests and a holy nation." The phrases "kingdom of priests and a holy nation" emphasize three core themes for understanding what it means to be God's people: mission, community, and holiness.

The rest of the Torah provides details for how God's people were to live faithfully. The remainder of this essay will explore these contours and reflect on the implications for ECP. We will follow broadly the Ten Commandments as a structure for summarizing Israel's ethic as Love God, Love Neighbor and Keep Sabbath.

Israel: God's New Humanity—Covenantal Living in Response to Grace

Jesus summarized the law by appealing to two broad statements drawn from the Torah (Matt 20:37–40; Mark 12:29–31; Luke 10:27): Love the Lord your God (Deut 6) and Love your neighbor as yourself (Lev 19:12).[10] We will use these two categories as headings for hearing the Old Testament's witness. We'll also explore the antitheses of loving God and loving neighbor = idolatry/syncretism and injustice. Last, we'll explore Sabbath as a core command that holds together the love of God and neighbor.

Loving God. The primary response to God's gracious actions is a singular devoted commitment to the Lord alone. Deuteronomy 6:4 reads, "The Lord is one" in the sense of being Israel's "one and only."[11] This phrase captures the sense of total allegiance and full person devotion. The Lord is qualitatively different and distinct from all other "gods" and relates to God's people via a relationship of undivided loyalty and devotion. The expected response to "The Lord is our one and only" (Deut 6:4) is a "full being" response of loving commitment and faithfulness. This is the sense of the command, "You will love the Lord your God with all your heart, soul, and strength" (Deut 6:5).

Israel's laws articulate frameworks for this devotion by prohibitions against the worship of other gods, the crafting of images, and using God's name in ways that dishonor God's character. The initial laws of the Ten Commandments summarize these prohibitions (Exod 20:2–7; cf. Deut 5:6–11). The other legal materials in the Torah offer more specific expansions of these prohibitions to guide God's people in faithful practices. The command to love God serves to emphasize the need for Church planters to ground their personal and

Means of Grace

business actions in a moment by moment relationship with the Lord. This will involve the implementation of habits and practices to sustain their commitment to their "One and Only."[12]

Antithesis: Danger of Idolatry. The antithesis of loving God is idolatry and syncretism. These options serve as warnings to ECP. As entrepreneurial church planters seek to gain traction in new contexts, they will encounter new philosophies, ideologies, and spiritualities. Like the ancient Israelites, the temptation will be to practice the worship of the Lord in ways that compromise the witness of God's people to the nations.[13]

Any reading of Israel's history recognizes the vast amount of material related to the ways that God's people practiced unfaithfulness to the Lord. From the Golden Calf (Exod 32–34) to Solomon's building of worship spaces for pagan wives (1 Kings 11:4–8) to the northern and southern kingdom's ongoing struggles with high places and false worship (1 Kgs 12–2 Kgs 25), there is an ongoing tension of engaging culture in contextually meaningful ways and crossing the line into a paganism that subverts the uniqueness of the LORD. Israel's prophets preach against the failings of God's people to practice a singular love for God apart from all others.[14]

The Old Testament has traditionally served as a bulwark against paganism.[15] It is critical for entrepreneurial church planters to heed the warnings that Israel's story provides of the pitfalls and dangers of being God's people in the midst of nations and cultures that do not yet know the Lord. The danger is the loss of the uniqueness of God vis-a-vis other gods, spiritualities, and philosophies. As Chris Wright observes, "[The gods] are *nothing is relation to YHWH; they are something in relation to their worshipers*" (italics in original).[16] The wise entrepreneurial church planter will be radically committed to engaging the culture evangelistically and economically while also being just as fully resolved to be faithful to God as his or her "One and Only."

Loving Neighbor. The second half of the Ten Commandments articulate broad categories for understanding how God's people are to relate with others: honoring parents, protecting life, guarding the sanctity of marriage, prohibiting theft, demanding truthfulness and integrity in legal matters, and banning the wrongful desire of people and property (20:12–17; cf. Deut 5:16–21). The Torah's other legal materials expand these to address issues of environmental justice, the treatment of marginalized persons (widows, orphans, poor, slaves, and immigrants), work, and the protection of consumers in business transactions (Exod

20:22–23:19; Lev 17:1–26:2; Deut 12:1–26:19).[17] The implications of Israel's ethic are clear. To confess the Lord as "One and Only" implies a holistic understanding of the world in which our vertical relationship with God informs and shapes our horizontal relationship with other people and the creation as a whole.[18] For the people of God, the ends do not justify the means. Witness is the paramount concern for the conduct of God's holy people. This has profound implications for ECP and helps to define one's business ethic. Its chief goal is not merely profit but an enterprise that indeed reflects God's character by how the conduct of the business witnesses to justice and love of neighbor at all levels of the entrepreneurial endeavor.

Antithesis: Injustice. Wherever the love of neighbor is absent, injustice is present in large and small ways. The Old Testament, especially its prophetic traditions, offer devastating critiques of the failings of God's people to extend justice to others, especially the marginalized. To cite one example, the prophet Amos in 5:10–13 lists a litany of abuses and injustices by the affluent in the northern Kingdom.[19] For ECP, the real risk in this model of launching new faith communities is the danger of injustice rearing its head in the conduct within the marketplace or in a lack of ministry among the marginalized and poor. The Torah's vision for justice ought to keep justice issues on the front burner for ECP whether the marketplaces engaged are in proximity to the poor or not. The call to "love neighbor" (Lev 19:18) involves embodying an ethic that extends God's blessings to the marginalized in society.

Sabbath. The Sabbath commandment stands at the center of the Ten Commandments (Exod 20:8–11; Deut 5:12–15 cf. Gen 2:1–3). Sabbath is the bridge between the commands regarding love for God and love for Neighbor. Sabbath first appears in Scripture as the climax of the first creation story (Gen 2:1–3). Its inclusion is particularly significant for ECP as both a witness and a warning.

Its function as testimony and witness to the true nature of reality is vital. Sabbath points to a different world and way of life than what human cultures cultivate. Sabbath shapes a distinct identity for God's people because it interrupts human activity and human generated attempts at productivity. It reminds us that human work is not the end or goal. Childs argues, "[I]t presupposes the cessation of the normal activity of work in order to set aside the sabbath for something special."[20]

It also testifies to the grace and goodness of God. Humans can't make or create a Sabbath. Our busy-ness will not manifest it. It is a gift from God. Janzen helpfully explains, "This is the paradox of grace, that the most important thing humans can do for God is to desist from trying to do anything…. The Sabbath is, above all, a call for humans to let God be God and to desist from all human attempts to manage the world through work and achievement, including religious work and achievement."[21]

Sabbath also offers a warning to ECP about the need for rest, renewal, and worship. By its nature, ECP is heavy in *human* activity. It assumes a vibrant participation in the marketplace *and* a commitment to missional witness. Either of these activities could easily consume a person's attention 24/7. Sabbath stands as a gift to a world focused on activity. Its message is clear. Work six days and dedicate the seventh to the Lord as a day of rest. It signals work and effort are not the highest values. Life does not advance from rest to work but from work to rest. This conception of time turns modern life on its head where rest and recreation merely serve as down time or off seasons in preparation for more action and work. Sabbath marks God's people with an identity apart from *work*. Sabbath is the end or goal. ECP is work done for God, but those who participate in this model must testify to the world that there is a God bigger than our world, our work, and even our calling. We witness to this by practicing Sabbath as part of our rhythm of life.[22] I'll give Abraham Heschel the final word:

> He who wants to enter the holiness of the day must first lay down the profanity of clattering commerce, of being yoked to toil. He must go away from the screech of dissonant days, from the nervousness and fury of acquisitiveness and the betrayal in embezzling his own life. He must say farewell to manual work and learn to understand that the world has already been created and will survive without the help of man. Six days a week we wrestle with the world, wringing profit from the earth; on the Sabbath we especially care for the seed of eternity planted in the soul. The world has our hands, but our soul belongs to Someone Else. Six days a week we seek to dominate the world, on the seventh day we try to dominate the self. [23]

Conclusion

The Old Testament has much to inform ECP in terms of the ethic that the Old Testament demands of God's people as they live out their missional calling of blessing others and reflecting God's character. he Old Testament provides key foundations for living as God's holy people in the midst of the nations in a way that demonstrates the reality of the one true God who is the "One and Only" of God's people. The closest analogies for the practice of ECP will be found in the New Testament, to which we now turn in the next chapter.

---

[1] Brevard S. Childs, *Old Testament Theology in a Canonical Context* (Minneapolis: Fortress, 1985), 108–54.

[2] For a missional understanding of the role of the Levitical priesthood, see Nicholas Haydock, *The Theology of the Levitical Priesthood: Assisting God's People in Their Mission to the Nations* (Eugene, OR: Wipf and Stock, 2015).

[3] All Scripture quotations are my own unless otherwise indicated.

[4] Michael Goheen, *A Light to the Nations: The Missional Church and the Biblical Story* (Grand Rapids: Academic, 2011); Brian D. Russell, *(re)Aligning with God: Reading Scripture for Church and World* (Eugene, OR: Cascade Books, 2015); and Christopher J. H. Wright, *The Mission of God: Unlocking the Bible's Grand Narrative* (Downers Grove, IL: IVP Academic, 2006).

[5] Walter Brueggemann, *Genesis*, Interpretation: A Bible Commentary for Teaching and Preaching (Louisville: John Knox, 1982), 31–35; Terence Fretheim, *God and the World in the Old Testament: A Relational Theology of Creation* (Nashville: Abingdon, 2005), 48–60; Cf. J. Richard Middleton, *The Liberating Image: The Imago Dei of Genesis 1* (Grand Rapids: Brazos, 2005).

[6] Bill T. Arnold, *Genesis*, The New Cambridge Bible Commentary (Cambridge: Cambridge University, 2009), 133; Richard Bauckham, *The Bible And Mission: Christian Witness in a Postmodern World* (Grand Rapids: Baker Academic, 2003), 28; Victor P. Hamilton, *The Book of Genesis: Chapters 1–17*, New International Commentary on the Old Testament (Grand Rapids: Eerdmans, 1990), 373–76; Cf. R. W.

L. Moberly *The Theology of the Book of Genesis* (Cambridge: Cambridge University Press, 2009), 141–61.

[7] I first heard Alex McManus articulate this principle in 2005 during an informal conversation in a coffeehouse in Ocoee, FL that served as an outreach for a faith community.

[8] For discuss of these phrases, see W. Ross Blackburn, *The God Who Makes Himself Known: The Missionary Heart of the Book of Exodus*, New Studies in Biblical Theology (Downers Grove, IL: IVP Academic, 2012), 89–95 and Russell, *(re)Aligning with God*, 42–43.

[9] This statement is so significant that it serves as the first commandment of the Ten Commandments according to Judaism.

[10] S. Dean McBride, Jr., "Yoke of the Kingdom: An Exposition of Deuteronomy 6:4–5," *Interpretation* 27.3 (1973): 273–304; Cf. Scott McKnight, *Jesus Creed: Loving God, Loving Others*, 10th anniversary ed. (Brewster, MA: Paraclete, 2014).

[11] R. W. L. Moberly, *Old Testament Theology: Reading the Hebrew Bible as Christian Scripture* (Grand Rapids: Baker Academic, 2013), 7–40 esp. 18–24. For the translation "one and only" compare Deut 6:4 with Song 6:9a.

[12] Ongoing reflection on Scripture is paramount: Deut 17:14–20; Josh 1:1–9; Ps 1, 19, and 119. Especially note the exhortation of constant meditation on the Torah in Josh 1:8 and Ps 1:3.

[13] Christopher J. H. Wright, "Reading the Old Testament Missionally" in *Reading the Bible Missionally*, ed. Michael W. Goheen (Grand Rapids: Eerdmans, 2016), 117–19.

[14] Russell, *(re)Aligning with God*, 64–65.

[15] G. Ernest Wright, *God Who Acts: Biblical Theology as Recital*, Studies in Biblical Theology 8 (London: SCM, 1952), 19–24. Cf. John D. Currid, *Against the Gods: The Polemical Theology of the Old Testament* (Wheaton, IL: Crossway, 2013); John Oswalt, *Called to Be Holy* (Nappanee, IN: Evangel, 1999), 9–20 and Wright, *Mission of God*, 136–88.

[16] Wright, *Mission of God*, 139.

[17] See literature on the Ten Commandments, the Book of the Covenant, and Deuteronomy for reflection on how the Ten Commandments inform and organize Israel's broader legal materials; Childs, *Old Testament Theology*, 63–83; Dean McBride, Jr., "Polity of the Covenant People: The Book of Deuteronomy," *Interpretation* 41.3 (1987): 229–44; Dennis Olson, "The Jagged Cliffs of Mount Sinai: A

Theological Reading of the Book of the Covenant (Exod 20:22–23:19)," *Interpretation* 50.3 (1996): 251–63; and Joe M. Sprinkle, "Law and Narrative in Exodus 19–24," *JETS* 47.2 (2004): 235–52.

[18] For broader discussions of Old Testament ethics, see Waldemar Janzen, *Old Testament Ethics: A Paradigmatic Approach* (Louisville: Westminster John Knox, 1994) and Christopher J. H. Wright, *Old Testament Ethics for the People of God* (Downers Grove, IL: IVP Academic, 2011).

[19] For reviews of the prophetic witness against injustice, see Bruce C. Birch, *Let Justice Roll Down: The Old Testament, Ethics, and the Christian Life* (Louisville: Westminster John Knox, 1991), 240–74.

[20] Brevard S. Childs, *The Book of Exodus: A Critical, Theological Commentary*, Old Testament Library (Louisville: Westminster John Knox, 1974), 416.

[21] Waldemar Janzen, *Exodus*, Believer's Church Bible Commentary (Harrisonburg, VA: Herald Press, 2000), 258.

[22] For a helpful contemporary reflection on Sabbath, see Dan B. Allender, *Sabbath*, Ancient Christian Practices (Nashville: Thomas Nelson, 2009).

[23] Abraham Heschel, *The Sabbath*. Introduction by Susannah Heschel. FSG Classics (New York: Farrar Straus Giroux, 2005), 13.

CHAPTER 3

The Business Behind and the Work Before Jesus

Fredrick J. Long

Introduction

Behind Jesus's ministry was business; before him was the work of the church. To work well was his witness, and he witnessed well by accomplishing his work. Not only did Jesus work as a young man in the trade of his earthly father, his teaching betrays a profound familiarity and interest in wealth, resources, and best business practices. At this time, the Galilee region was relatively stable and enjoyed a growing commerce in fishing, agriculture, olive oil, and supplying resources for large city-scale building projects. It was within this context that Jesus announced the inbreaking of God's Kingdom and his fulfillment of Isaiah's vision of the Jubilee year. Jesus affirmed the value of work; he transformed both work in business and the work of proclaiming the good news of God's kingdom.

Importantly, Jesus surrounded himself with men (at least five) who worked in two other prominent regional businesses—fishing and tax collecting. Additionally, an entourage of women followers was serving Jesus financially by giving out of their own resources; they reflected Kingdom values of gracious giving in response to God's grace. Importantly, Jesus's ministry and discipleship were not anti-business; rather, in agreement with the Jewish Scripture and culture, Jesus valued good work and beneficial business and encouraged these in his teachings. Although ancient business "opportunities" were much different than ours in many countries today, Jesus promoted just and gracious business practices that reflected both the business perspective of equity, opportunity, and justice as well as the worker's perspective to face challenges, think creatively, be persistent, persevere, and undertake constructive labor.

I'd like to address three problematic views (some even prevalent myths) about the context of Jesus's life and ministry in the Galilee. The discussion that follows will be organized by my further treatment of these topics.

1. <u>Myth 1</u>: *The Galilee region was destitute, the backwaters of Judea, with numerous gentiles.* Rather, the Galilee was a politically stable agricultural region with a growing diverse commerce (fishing, textiles, pottery, olive oil) invigorated by the new construction of Roman-planned cities like Sepphoris and Tiberius founded by Herod Antipas. Moreover, the region was largely inhabited by Jews who interacted faithfully and commercially with gentiles in the Galilee and in the Decapolis region on the eastern shores.[1]

2. <u>Myth 2</u>: *Jesus was a poor carpenter.* Rather, he was a builder who worked with stone and wood in the construction of buildings. Jesus's teaching betrays an extensive knowledge of building in general rather than simply woodworking.[2] Moreover, his family was not in the lower economic tiers but more towards the middle of the broad economic spectrum.

3. <u>Myth 3</u>: *Jesus's elevation of the vocation of ministry relegated the business and government vocations as second rate.* Rather, Jesus affirmed each sphere of vocation even as he advanced a new movement under the jurisdiction of the Kingdom of God and prepared new disciples for this movement. Jesus had new wine and needed new wineskins.

Galilee

The Galilee region was to the north of Roman controlled Judea under the political control of Herod Antipas in Jesus's day. The region comprised two thousand square miles. According to the Jewish historian Josephus, a Jewish general of the Galilee captured early in the Jewish War with Rome, it had an estimated population of two to three million people.[3] These figures are too high, and yet the Galilee contained over two hundred towns and many thousands of agricultural workers were needed year-round.

Josephus described the fertility of the Galilee and the surrounding region in quite glowing terms (*JW* 3.506–21). The sea contained all kinds of fish, one of which he identifies as the coracin fish, "undoubtedly a Cichlid of the genus *Tilapia.*"[4] The northern city Bethsaida was known as "a house of fish" and the city "Tarichea on the south was a fish factory"[5] from the Greek ταριχεῖαι meaning "factories for salting fish."[6] This latter town was called in Hebrew *Magdala Nunayya* "Magdala of the Fishes," the hometown of Mary Magdalene.[7] Josephus described that the land was "so fruitful that all sorts of trees can grow upon it, and the inhabitants accordingly plant all sorts of trees there"—walnut, palm, balsam, fig, etc. Moreover, the land "not only nourishes different sorts of autumnal fruit beyond men's expectation, but preserves them a great while; it supplies men with the principal fruits, with grapes and figs continually during ten months of the year, and the rest of the fruit as they become ripe together, through the whole year."[8] Also found there were pomegranates, olives, and various grains, including flax.

Upper Galilee in the north was more Jewish with the two most important cities being Capernaum and Bethsaida. Lower Galilee had more Greco-Roman influence; Nazareth was located there and less than four miles away lay Sepphoris along two major roadways. Herod Antipas had rebuilt Sepphoris, which was the government seat of Galilee until Herod finished building the city Tiberius around AD 19-20 along the sea that was renamed after the emperor (John 6:1; 21:1).[9] The artistic and Roman construction of these two major cities encouraged commerce and brought relative wealth, stability, and even significant growth as is attested in the notable increase of settlements in the region.[10] Likewise, excavations of villages confirm this growth and the presence of various businesses. For example, Cana enjoyed oil and textile production and glass blowing; Yodefat produced olive oil, pottery, and textiles; and Gamla had a commercial neighborhood with an olive oil extraction plant, flourmill, and shops.[11] Thus, Morten Hørning Jensen is justified to conclude, "in the villages the ancient Galileans to a certain extent cultivated what grew best on their farming plots and relied on trade and markets in the cities to supply their other needs. Urban-rural relations were seemingly more reciprocal than has been argued from time to time."[12] Helping the transport of goods were port cities along the western Mediterranean coast, such as Lydda, Joppa, Caesarea and further north Ptolemais, Tyre, Sidon, and Antioch.

For these reasons, the Galilee was a crossroads of commerce being "crisscrossed by major trading routes between east and west that ensured it would never be isolated from the wider life of the empire. Here Jesus would meet and mix with many people who were not Jewish, and he no doubt spent much of his time thinking and talking about the ideas of the Greeks and Romans as well as the religious heritage of his own people."[13] Jesus's base of operation, Capernaum on the Sea of the Galilee, had great capacity for business with a population of around ten thousand, a Roman outpost (Matt 8:5–13), and a customs station (Matt 2:14).[14] The Galilee provided the context and content for Jesus's parables and miracles: 19 of 32 recorded parables were spoken here and 25 of 33 recorded miracles were performed here.[15] Thus, the commercial environment of the Galilee provides a critical context for understanding Jesus's upbringing and trade (immediately below) and his understanding of vocation and work (see "Jesus's Jubilee, Vocation, and Work" further below).

Jesus's Upbringing and Trade

Jesus's family belonged to something akin to the working middle class, which affected his teaching.[16] Although the Gospels contain no direct account of Jesus working in a business, those from his home town, puzzled about his "job change," asked, "Is not this the builder [τέκτων], the son of Mary, and brother of James and Joses and Judas and Simon? Are not his sisters here with us?" (Mark 6:3, my translation). The rhetorical question in Greek expects a "yes" answer. Mark concludes, "and they took offense at Him." Matthew's account has, "Is not this the builder's son?" (Matt 13:55). Implied here is that Jesus, like typical sons, learned his father's trade.

A τέκτων was a builder, most often working with stone and wood.[17] The apocryphal *Gospel of James* 9.3 from the second-century indicated that Joseph constructed buildings.[18] As seen above, the Galilee of Jesus's day in the environs of Nazareth enjoyed both an active agricultural industry and large building projects; the reconstructed town of Sepphoris was actively being built while Jesus was apprenticing as a builder under his father. It is not unreasonable to think that Joseph and Jesus walked to Sepphoris and back (one hour each way) to work on the various construction projects there.[19] Klaus

Dieter Issler rightly calculates that Jesus worked in the construction ministry for at least eighteen years (between the ages of twelve and thirty) before officially starting his proclamation that the Kingdom of God has arrived.[20]

In this respect, Jesus's knowledge of building practices is immense and supports this view. Ken M. Campbell indicates that Jesus's description of "everyday life … referred to human activities: eating and drinking, commerce, agriculture, and especially building." For the latter, among the numerous examples organized and provided by Campbell are these: building (Luke 17:28), barns (Luke 12:18), watch towers (Matt 21:33; Luke 13:4; 14:28–30), vineyards (Matt 20:1), houses (Matt 7:24–27; John 14:1–14), palaces (Luke 7:25), inns (Luke 10:34), temples (Matt 23:35; John 2:21), embankments (Luke 19:43–44), cities (Matt 5:14); parts of houses such as rooftops (Matt 10:27; 24:17), the inner (private) room (Luke 12:3), storerooms (Matt 13:52), upper-level rooms (Mark 14:15), guest rooms in large dwellings (Luke 22:11), wedding halls (Matt 22:10), courtyards (Matt 26:3; John 10:16), home security (Matt 12:29; 24:43); clay ovens (Matt 6:30), kilns (Matt 13:42, 50), toilets (Matt 15:17), tombs (Matt 23:27–29), millstones (Matt 18:6; Luke 17:1–2), barricades (Luke 19:43), fences (Matt 21:38), animal stalls (Luke 13:15), wells (Luke 14:5), entrances (John 10:9), gates (Matt 7:13–14), threshing floors (Matt 3:12), wine presses (Matt 21:33), and wine troughs (Matt 12:1). Interestingly, we find only a few references to wood: the beam/splinter (Matt 7:3–5), wet vs. dry wood (Luke 23:31), and perhaps (wooden) gates (Matt 7:13–14). Yet even these references betray construction. Campbell concludes, "In light of all this knowledge of the building trade it is hard to resist the conclusion that Jesus was involved in construction."[21] How did Jesus's work experience affect his understanding of vocation and work? How did his life relate to Hebrew Scripture?

Jesus's Jubilee, Vocation, and Work

Foundational for Jesus's understanding of his vocation is his fulfillment of Scripture, specifically Isaiah's vision of the Jubilee year fulfilled. In Luke 4:18–19 at the synagogue in Nazareth, we see the beginning of Jesus's public ministry where he read aloud Isaiah 61:1–2 and announced the fulfillment of Isaiah's Jubilee, the favorable year of the Lord, that he himself inaugurated:

18 "THE SPIRIT OF THE LORD IS UPON ME,
    BECAUSE HE ANOINTED ME TO PREACH THE GOSPEL
    TO THE POOR.
    HE HAS SENT ME TO PROCLAIM RELEASE TO THE
    CAPTIVES,
    AND RECOVERY OF SIGHT TO THE BLIND,
    TO SET FREE THOSE WHO ARE OPPRESSED,
19 TO PROCLAIM THE FAVORABLE YEAR OF THE LORD."[22]

Jesus concluded the statement saying, "Today this Scripture has been fulfilled in your hearing" (Luke 4:21). Isaiah described here an eschatological Jubilee, "the favorable year of the Lord." The Jubilee year is described in Leviticus 25 and was to be announced every fiftieth year throughout the land of Israel on the Day of Atonement (Lev 25:9). It is uncertain to what extent Isaiah and Jesus envisioned the Jubilee to be realized, but Jesus nevertheless announced its Isaian fulfillment in his coming. Leviticus proscribed that any land/property lost due to the need to sell it would be returned to the original family so that they would work it once again. Rather than holding tight to land holdings and squeezing out all that one could gain at the expense of others, the Jubilee celebrated renewed opportunity for all of God's people to work their own land for their own benefit. The Jubilee year released people from their debt burdens in order to pursue productive work and offer goods and services. In the Intertestamental period, kings proclaimed the forgiveness of both sins and monetary debts at the start of their reigns "in order to unseat the wealthy and gain favor with the poor" as, for example, Ptolemy VIII in Egypt.[23] The Intertestamental Jewish Qumran community (second-century BC to mid-first-century AD) expected a Melchizedek messianic figure who would come and fulfill the Jubilee Year (11QMelchizedek).

    Possibly influenced by the teaching tradition at Qumran, John the Baptist announced the forgiveness of sins to prepare for Jesus's coming (Mark 1:4//Luke 3:2). In the Gospels of Matthew and Mark, Jesus brought with him the beginning of the reign of God's Kingdom announcing, "Repent for the Kingdom of God is at hand" (Matt 4:17//Mark 1:15). Yet, such a direct statement from the mouth of Jesus is not found in Luke's Gospel, instead, Luke initiates Jesus's ministry with his reading of Isaiah and fulfilling the Jubilee Year described there. Subsequently in Luke's Gospel, we observe repeated statements and allusions showing that Isaiah's Jubilee is fulfilled among especially the poor who receive favor and the good news of Jesus (Luke 6:20; 7:22; 14:21; 16:20, 22; 18:22; 19:8; 21:3). Not surprisingly, Jesus's actions fulfilling Isaiah's Jubilee—in healing, proclamation, and addressing the needs of the poor—are matched by Jesus's teaching about the financial and business values of the Kingdom, especially his parables (addressed in the next chapter).

Before looking at Jesus's parables, it is important for us to define some terms relating to "work."[24] According to Dallas Willard, a "job" is something for which a person obtains resources for sustenance of life; "ministry" is that which God has entrusted each person to do specially and specifically; "work" consists of the totality of what a person does and acquires, thus encompassing job and ministry; and one's "life" is all that he or she is encompassing one's job, ministry, and work.[25] Recent attention has been devoted to think about and describe "work" in relation to the Christian faith.[26] In this regard, Darrell Cosden provides a very helpful definition of work:

> Human work is a transformative activity essentially consisting of dynamically interrelated instrumental, relational, and onto-logical dimensions: whereby, along with work being an end in itself [*ontological*], the worker's and others' needs are providen-tially met; believers' sanctification is occasioned [*instrumental*]; and workers express, explore and develop their humanness while building up their natural, social and cultural environ-ments thereby contributing protectively and productively to the order of this world and the one to come [*relational*].[27]

In short, you can remove a person from work but you cannot remove work from the person. Humans are created for productive, dignifying, satisfying, and God-honoring work.

For our purposes here, it is particularly important to understand that Jesus embodied work in his life in the proper sense of the word "work" as Cosden defines it. John's Gospel is particularly helpful here since "work" and "deeds" are repeated themes. For Jesus, to accomplish God's will and do this work was his "food" (John 4:34; cf. 5:20, 36; 17:4; 19:28, 30). For other people, their work is simply to trust God (John 6:28–29), and specifically to accept that Jesus is food/bread from heaven (John 6:30–69; 14:10–13); importantly, this is in the context of miraculously feeding the needy people (John 6:1–14, 26). Moreover, Jesus spoke favorably about participating in the work accomplished by others (John 4:35–38)—in context, this work is the Samaritan woman's testimony about Jesus (John 4:28–30, 39–42). Here Jesus metaphorically overlaid "harvesting work" with "evangelism work" (as in Matt 9:37–38) much like he overlaid eating real bread with eating himself (John 6), and "fishing work" to catching humans as "fishers of people" (Mark 1:17).[28] Here we must be careful: Rather than interpreting the purpose of Jesus's metaphors to subordinate or even replace income-earning jobs with evangelism work, it is better to understand Jesus's purpose to invigorate the work of evangelism with the positive valuation of basic human needs (food) and needed income-earning jobs; both business and evangelism are productive types of work. Indeed, both are work providing sustenance—physically and spiritually. In other words, our necessary and daily work of gaining sustenance metaphorically maps onto our work of believing and helping others come to believe (evangelism). Evangelism thus is infused with the value of honest and good labor, *which does not in any way diminish physical labor, but rather properly values it.* So, rather than disassociating our jobs from the Gospel, Jesus has effectively merged them such that, first, evangelism has the value of sustenance-producing work and, second, our jobs may be seen as ministry and participating in the work of God across our life. To this latter point, Ken Eldred helps to articulate three aspects of our ministry in working our jobs:

1. a ministry *at* work: pointing those around us to God (evangelistic witness)
2. a ministry *of* work: serving and creating via work itself (productivity in our jobs)
3. a ministry *to* work: redeeming the practices, policies and structures of institutions (converting our jobs to reflect Kingdom values of ministry).[29]

What this means is that *all of our human work* in the gospel of Jesus is redeemed by Jesus's fulfillment of Isaiah's vision of Jubilee.

In this regard, Issler helpfully distinguishes different job sectors present today that also existed in Jesus's day: "*public* (working for government), *private not-for-profit* (civic, moral, and religious organizations that rely on donations for all or part of their operating budgets), and *private for-profit* (various small and large businesses in the market-place)."[30] Issler argues rightly that Jesus clearly valued work in each sector. For example, Jesus accepted the role of public government which believers support by paying taxes (Matt 17:24–25; 22:17–21; cf. Rom 13:1–7). This does not mean, however, that each sector is immune from critique—Jesus indeed critiqued each sector. For example, Jesus commanded his disciples not to be like those serving in governmental public capacities who "lord it over the people" who are called "benefactors" (Luke 22:25–26). At issue here is that political-financial benefactors take the place of God and are so worshipped by the people. Political leaders then (i.e., the imperial cult) and now may be idolized such that they become objects of worship to be imitated. Jesus instead offered himself as an example to follow. Also, Jesus powerfully critiqued the religious leadership (priesthood, scribes, and Pharisees) in Mark 11–12.[31] Such prophetic critique resulted in the authorities crucifying Jesus; he understood this would happen when he travelled fatefully to Jerusalem to prophetically confront the religious/national authorities (Mark 8:30–31; 9:30–31; 10:32–34). Likewise, John the Baptist admonished soldiers not to use force and take money, not to falsely accuse ("to receive bribes" is implied), but rather to be content with their pay; also, tax collectors were not to collect more than they had been ordered to (Luke 3:12–14). Thus, the message of the Kingdom infiltrated into each sector of work in Jesus's day, even as is needed today.

Conclusion

Jesus's life in the Galilee exposed him to the value of good labor and seeing this work from the perspective of having negotiated business commerce and faithfulness to God. In fulfilling God's purposes, Jesus understood Isaiah's vision of the Jubilee year to be present. Under God's Kingdom, debts are to be forgiven, land returned, good work restored, the sick healed, and the good news preached to the poor. This fulfillment is demonstrated in Jesus's life of service and in his teaching that views both work and ministry as valuable if not even interrelated. Many of Jesus's parables involve or imply business settings, the investment of resources, and human workers. In the next chapter, we will look at these parables and the early church's appropriation of Jesus's teaching in order to guide entrepreneurial church planters today to interrelate their work and ministry, as Jesus's encouraged.

[1] Morten Hørning Jensen, "Rural Galilee and Rapid Changes: An Investigation of the Socio-Economic Dynamics and Developments in Roman Galilee," *Biblica* 93.1 (2012): 43–67.

[2] See the excellent review in Ken M. Campbell, "What Was Jesus' Occupation?" *JETS* 48 (2005): 501–19, and his conclusions on p. 512.

[3] A of number 3,000,000 may be arrived at by multiplying Josephus's claim that there were 204 towns in the Galilee (probably correct) with the smallest having 15,000 people (incorrect).

[4] Theodore Gill, *Contributions to the Life Histories of Fishes* (Washington: Smithsonian Institution, 1909), 518.

[5] Spiros Zodhiates, "Γαλιλαία," *The Complete Word Study Dictionary: New Testament* (Chattanooga, TN: AMG, 2000), s.v.

[6] Henry George Liddell et al., *A Greek-English Lexicon* (Oxford: Clarendon, 1996), 1758.

[7] August Merk, "Magdala," *The Catholic Encyclopedia*, Vol. 9 (New York: Robert Appleton, 1910), accessed 28 Nov. 2017 <http://www.newadvent.org/cathen/09523a.htm>.

[8] William Whiston, trans., *The Works of Josephus: Complete and Unabridged* (Peabody, MA: Hendrickson, 1987), 662.

[9] Jordan Ryan, "Tiberias," *The Lexham Bible Dictionary* (Bellingham, WA: Lexham, 2016), np

[10] See Jensen, "Rural Galilee," 50–55.

[11] Jensen, "Rural Galilee," 58–59.

[12] Jensen, "Rural Galilee," 61.

[13] John William Drane, *Introducing the New Testament*, rev. ed. (Oxford: Lion, 2000), 51.

[14] R. T. France, *The Gospel of Mark: A Commentary on the Greek Text*. New International Greek Testament Commentary (Grand Rapids: Eerdmans, 2002), 101.

[15] Henry W. Holloman, "Galilee, Galileans," *Baker Encyclopedia of the Bible* (Grand Rapids: Baker, 1988), 836.

[16] Campbell, "What Was Jesus' Occupation?," 517. Campbell, surveying Jesus's language concludes, "this teaching by Jesus has more affinity with what are now called 'middle-class values' than with any revolutionary agenda! While this may be unwelcome news to some interpreters, this perception is strengthened when we consider his references to management and employment."

[17] See BDAG, s.v. and James Hope Moulton and George Milligan, *The Vocabulary of the Greek Testament* (London: Hodder and Stoughton, 1930), 628–29.

[18] In some tension with this is Justin Martyr in the mid second-century who indicated that Jesus when living among people made "plows and yokes, teaching through these *both* the symbols of righteousness/justice *and* an active mode of life" (*Dialogue* 88.8, my translation). Justin clearly valued the work that Jesus engaged in and understood it as peaceable. But how did Jesus making plows and yokes symbolize righteousness? In context and elsewhere, Justin explains that Jesus and the Word of God spreading forth from Jerusalem fulfills Isa 6:3–4 (cf. Micah 4:1–3) in which the nations are taught to turn away from the sword and warfare towards peace and converting their swords to plowshares (*First Apology* 39.1; *Dialogue* 109.2; 110.3). However, as a builder in construction, Jesus could also make farming implements. Also, it is clear that Justin's view of Jesus's occupational focus on plows is informed by his understanding of Jesus fulfilling Isaiah 6:3–4 to bring peace.

[19] Eric Meyers, "Jesus Probably Trilingual" transcript from *Jesus' Social Class* produced for Frontline at https://www.pbs.org/wgbh/pages/frontline/shows/religion/jesus/socialclass.html accessed 12-12-2017. Meyers says, "It's very likely that Jesus actually worked in Sepphoris in the time of Antipas' activity there. Of that there's probably no doubt."

[20] Klaus Dieter Issler, *Living into the Life of Jesus: The Formation of Christian Character* (Downers Grove, IL: IVP, 2012), 190.

[21] Campbell, "What Was Jesus' Occupation?," 517–18, with quote at 518. I have removed the Greek words that Campbell supplies and slightly edited these lists.

[22] From this point onward, all Scripture quotations, unless otherwise indicated, are from the *New American Standard Bible: 1995 Update* (La Habra, CA: The Lockman Foundation, 1995).

[23] Lois Tverberg, *Reading the Bible with Rabbi Jesus: How a Jewish Perspective can Transform your Understanding* (Grand Rapids: BakerBooks, 2017), 227. I am indebted to Tverberg to investigate Jubilee with the coming Messiah as seen in the Qumran *Pesher* document 11QMelchizedek.

[24] I am particularly indebted in this section to the discussion and sources used by Issler, *Living into the Life of Jesus*, 184–221.

[25] Dallas Willard, "*Some Steps Toward Soul Rest* in Eternal Living," Biola University Faculty Workshop, August 17, 2011, summarized and discussed in Issler, *Living into the Life of Jesus*, 186.

[26] In addition to the works cited in this essay, see, e.g., the Institute for Faith, Work, and Economics and the resources offered there at https://tifwe.org/resource/. See also Issler, *Living into the Life of Jesus*, 185n4; he mentions these books: Michael Novak, *Business as a Calling: Work and the Examined Life* (New York: Free Press, 1996), John Schneider, *The Good of Affluence* (Grand Rapids: Eerdmans, 2002); Wayne Grudem, *Business for the Glory of God* (Wheaton, IL: Crossway, 2003); Kenman Wong and Scott Rae, *Business for the Common Good: A Christian Perspective for the Marketplace* (Downers Grove, IL: InterVarsity, 2011).

[27] Darrell Cosden, *A Theology of Work* (Eugene, OR: Wipf & Stock, 2006), 178–79.

[28] For a discussion of this metaphor and its implications, see Blake Wassell and Stephen Llewelyn, "'Fishers of Humans,' the Contemporary Theory of Metaphor, and Conceptual Blending Theory," *JBL* 133 (2014): 627–46.

[29] Ken Eldred, *The Integrated Life* (Montrose, CO: Manna, 2010), 107. These three items with italicized prepositions were found in Issler, *Living into the Life of Jesus*, 195. I have added the parenthetical comments.

[30] Issler, *Living into the Life of Jesus*, 189.

[31] See Mark A. Awabdy and Fredrick J. Long, "Mark's Inclusion of 'For All Nations' in 11:17d and the International Vision of Isaiah," *The Journal of Inductive Biblical Studies* 1.2 (2014): 224–55 available at http://place.asburyseminary. edu/jibs/vol1/iss2/5/ and Benson Goh, "The Charge of Being Deluded Interpreters of Scripture: A Reassessment of the Importance of Chiasms in Mark 11–12," *The Journal of Inductive Biblical Studies* 2.1 (2015): 30–61 available at http://place.asburyseminary.edu/jibs/vol2/iss1/4/.

CHAPTER 4

Jesus's Entrepreneurial Teaching and His Earliest Disciples

Fredrick J. Long

Introduction

Instrumentally, Jesus's teaching and discipleship laid the foundation for the growth and expansion of the first churches in the New Testament era. The inspirational framework that he provided is perceived in the particulars of his teaching ministry and the instructions for his earliest disciples. While proclaiming the Gospel, Jesus and his disciples had a money pouch for meeting the needs of the poor (John 12:6; 13:29). When faced with the need to feed a large crowd, the disciples offered seven months pay presumably out of their own means to purchase food for the crowds (Luke 9:13//Mark 6:37). While Herod Antipas was throwing a banquet "for his lords and military commander and leading men of Galilee" (Mark 6:21), the poor crowds found Jesus who took on the mantel of the Shepherd for them as his sheep and taught and fed them (Mark 6:34–44; cf. Mark 8:1–9). In this manner, Jesus with his disciples forged a new way of being in the world even as the world as they knew it would soon come crashing to an end with the Jewish War of AD 70.

In this chapter, I will address three problematic views (some even prevalent myths) about Jesus's teaching and the life of discipleship of the first believers, especially Peter. The discussion that follows will be organized by my further treatment of these topics.

1. <u>Myth 1</u>: *Many of Jesus's teachings and parables involved money and thus he taught against wealth.* Rather, Jesus taught about the relative value of wealth and its dangers. Positively, Jesus urged its gracious and responsible use as well as the forgiveness of debts.

2. <u>Myth 2</u>: *Jesus's disciples were poor, inexperienced young men.* Rather, we know that Peter was married and Jesus stayed in his house (Mark 1:29–30). Moreover, Peter and Andrew worked together with James and John in a family fishing business that had hired hands (Luke 5:10; Mark 1:20). Also, Matthew (Levi) was a tax collector. These men were located in the middle of the economic spectrum. Additionally, Jesus was served graciously by women followers, such as Joanna who was very well-connected to Herod the Tetrarch in the Galilee and had access to resources. These women shared their resources presumably acquired through their industry (Luke 8:1–4). Business supported Jesus's work.

3. <u>Myth 3</u>: *After Jesus's crucifixion and resurrection, the disciples foolishly "reverted" back to their business of fishing (John 21:2–3), thus rejecting Jesus's teaching.* Although Jesus points to their failure to catch fish and they understood this,[1] he then helped them succeed with a good catch and proceeded to prepare a meal and encouraged them, especially Peter, whom he commanded to "feed the sheep" (John 21:15–17).

I will address each of these myths in further detail throughout the rest of this chapter in order to paint an accurate picture of Jesus perspective on entrepreneurship among his earliest disciples.

Jesus's Teachings—Wealth and Business

Large portions of Jesus's teachings concern money, and from this fact, it is too often concluded that working for wealth is bad. Well, it depends on what the wealth is used for and whether or not one is compromised ethically while working for wealth. Jesus taught that one cannot serve both God and wealth/mammon; one must choose (Matt 6:24). In this respect, Jesus aligned with the Jewish Scripture's prophetic critique of Israel's rich rulers abusing the people like shepherds ravaging their own sheep, feeding themselves and not the sheep (Ezek 34). Rather, one should be generous with resources and beware of every form of greed (Luke 12:15); one should loan to the one asking to borrow from you (Matt 5:42); if wealthy, one should not build more storage units to accumulate more wealth (Luke 12:16–21) but rather steward one's possessions to also consider the needs of others, especially the poor (Luke 12:33; Matt 19:16–22).

What about business? Importantly, Jesus was not anti-business. Especially relevant here are twenty-four of Jesus's thirty-seven parables that involve business settings and the proper use of wealth and resources.[2] We can learn much by studying these parables. In the following chart, I describe the **Business Values** and the *Kingdom Message* of these parables progressively as found in Luke's Gospel (sixteen) followed by those found only in the Gospels of Matthew (seven) or Mark (one). I have summarized Luke's version if the parable is found in more than one Gospel.

Parables of Jesus within a Business Setting	Business Values & *Kingdom Message*
New Wine into Old Wineskins (Luke 5:37–39; Matt 9:17–17; Mark 2:21–22)	**New wine requires flexible new packaging**; *the disciples are the new packaging to receive and convey Jesus's Message of the Kingdom.*
The Wise vs. Foolish Builders (Luke 6:46–49; Matt 7:24–27)	**Proper/wise construction relies on a proper foundation**; *a proper foundation is obeying Jesus's teaching.*
The Two Debtors (Luke 7:41–43)	**People love having their debts forgiven, esp. big ones;** *God forgives our debts, and the more debt we acknowledge we owed, the more thankful we will be.*
Parable of the Sower (Luke 8:5–8; Matt 13:3–9; Mark 4:3–9)	**Sowing generously, if not even indiscriminately, provides a great return despite some failure**; *the Word of God does not discriminate but produces great fruit where it finds a fully receptive place in honest, good, persevering hearts.*
The Rich Fool (Luke 12:15–21, 33–34)	**Business success should not be for storing up wealth for oneself, but for being rich towards God**; *avoid every form of greed, sell one's possessions ("excess" implied), and give to charity; one's heart is where one's treasure is.*

The Faithful House Manager (Luke 12:35–48; Matt 24:42–51; Mark 13:34–37)	**Slaves should faithfully serve their masters even when absent and will be rewarded with greater responsibility, and if disobedient, will be punished;** *Jesus's followers should be faithfully serving him even when absent to the degree that they have been entrusted much by him, or, (it is implied) they will await punishment.*
The Barren Fig Tree (Luke 13:5–9)	**Trees (and businesses) take time to grow and may require specific, radical care to produce fruit; but if not, then they may need to removed;** *the fruit of repentance in response to the Word of God is expected or else one will perish.*
The Great Banquet (Luke 14:16–24; Matt 22:1–14)	**Business activities may remove one from experiencing kingdom fellowship; those most in need of the provision of fellowship are the poor, crippled, lame, blind, and travelers/foreigners;** *the poor, crippled, lame, blind, and the travelers/foreigners are included in God's Kingdom when those first invited fail to attend due to worldly priorities.*
Tower Builder (Luke 14:28–33)	**Projects must be planned and financially paid for or else they will not be finished;** *being Jesus's disciple requires relinquishment of selfish control of all one's possessions.*
The Lost Sheep (Luke 15:3–7; Matt 18:10–14)	**Valuable business assets that are lost should be (eagerly) sought after;** *lost sinners are valuable to God, eagerly sought after, and found with great joy.*
The Prodigal & Resentful Sons (Luke 15:11–32)	**Desperate people agree to objectionable labor and are maltreated; however, rebellious but then repentant sons should be welcomed back into the family and its business;** *God happily receives back sinners even while others may be resentful of this.*
The Unjust Steward (Luke 16:1–13)	**Squandering a boss's resources is an unacceptable business practice, yet using business resources generously may bestow honor to the business owner;** *use wealth to befriend people to obtain eternal dwellings/reward.*[9]

The Master and Servant (Luke 17:7–10)	**A master commands his servants/slaves to tend to his needs before their own needs;** *disciples are like servants in needing to obey the Lord as expected.*
Pharisee and the Tax Collector (Luke 18:9–14)	**Although some professions seem more godly than others, one should avoid stereo-typing and judging people on this basis;** *"everyone exalting him- or herself will be humbled but the one humbling him- or herself will be exalted."*
The Talents or Minas (Luke 19:12–27; Matt 25:14–30)	**To obtain a business return, one must invest resources: The reward is proportional to the investment, and the degree of faithful success is proportional to the greater responsibilities offered;** "to everyone who has 'faithful action' [implied], more shall be given, but from the one who does not have 'faithful action' [implied], even what he does have shall be taken away."
The Wicked Tenants (Luke 20:9–16; Matt 21:33–41; Mark 12:1–9)	**Land tenants (vine-growers) do not work for their own harvest, but for the owner's harvest;** *God expected the leaders of Israel to produce Kingdom fruit in Israel, but they generally rejected God's ways, so consequently God will punish the leaders and give its leadership to others.*
The Tares (Matt 13:24–30)	**The business (of sowing) may encounter an enemy's sabotage (of weeds), but one should trust in the final good outcome when the good business is separated from the bad;** *God sows his sons and daughters into the world and the devil also has sown enemies as stumbling blocks and lawless people, but in the final judgement, these two groups will be distinguished and judged in kind.*
The Field of Treasure (Matt 13:44)	**A person accidentally finding a great treasure on a property sells all to buy the property;** *the Kingdom of God is like this.*
Parable of the Pearl (Matt 13:45–46)	**A merchant seeks very valuable things and wisely acquires them with great cost;** *the Kingdom of God is like such a merchant.*

Drawing in the Net (Matt 13:47–50)	**Fishing with nets is indiscriminate until the end when the bad fish are removed;** *the Kingdom of God is like this when the angels remove the wicked from the righteous and cast them into the fiery furnace with weeping/great regret.*
The Unforgiving Servant (Matt 18:23–35)	**One receiving compassionate forgiveness of debt should forgive others their debt; otherwise, that person will be considered wicked and will be punished;** *God will punish each of us who do not forgive each other from the heart.*
The Workers in the Vineyard (Matt 20:1–16)	**Hiring and payment practices should be "good/generous," even offering latecomers their needed daily provision;** *the Kingdom of God is like this.*
The Two Sons Working the Vineyard (Matt 21:28–32)	**Sons committing to work should work the family business. It is better to work than not to work, even if one initially refused to work;** *the tax collectors and prostitutes believed the Gospel, but the chief priests and elders did not believe, nor did they change their minds subsequently.*
The Growing Seed (Mark 4:26–29)	**The sowing, growing, and reaping of crops is a wonderful and mysterious process;** *the Kingdom of God is like this.*

It is surprising how consistently business values, principles, and practices may be discerned in the parables that, true, primarily serve as vehicles for Jesus's Kingdom message that is summarized so well by Klyne R. Snodgrass,

> The primary focus of the parables is the coming of the kingdom of God and the resulting discipleship that is required. When Jesus proclaimed the kingdom he meant that God was exercising his power and rule to bring forgiveness, defeat evil and establish righteousness in fulfillment of the OT promises. In Jesus' own person and ministry these acts were happening, and the kingdom was made available to people. The kingdom comes with limitless grace, but with it comes limitless demand. That is why it is impossible to speak of the kingdom without at the same time speaking of discipleship.[4]

The question remains, however, "Why did Jesus choose the context of business/work/resources as a metaphoric vehicle and literary framework for a majority of his parables that carried his Kingdom message?"

I would maintain that Jesus did so to show how the Kingdom intersects with these foundational facets of life in God's World—how work, business, and the use of resources are to be seen in view of the Kingdom. Work is foundational to human life as is earning benefit, reward, and wealth in that work. The pressing question is, however, "Within which framework are work and wealth best understood and lived?" Jesus clearly provided the answer: the in-breaking Kingdom of God that fulfills Isaiah's Jubilee vision. In this respect, Jesus's teaching would have been particularly poignant for his twelve disciples who had worked within important (provision of food), if not even, controversial jobs (e.g., Matthew's tax collecting). In general, these parables involving business settings show that Jesus in fact supported fair, wise, honest, honorable, and gracious uses of financial resources and business practices. The Kingdom of God was available to people in the midst of their work and business. Righteousness—that is, rightly relating to one another in just and fair practices—is revealed in Jesus's teaching. By overlaying the truths of the Kingdom onto business and work places (fields, homes, lakes, construction sites, etc.) and relationships (family, servants/masters, co-workers), Jesus was viewing and honoring work and business from the perspective of the Kingdom. Discipleship in Jesus means transformed work and business in view of the Kingdom. People can then find their missional calling inside their existing work and not simply outside of it.

The Twelve Apostles and other Disciples

What was Jesus's goal in calling disciples from among those working in professions? It is intriguing that he chose some "fishermen" and then seizes on their work as a metaphor "fishers of people" for what work he would have them do: proclaim the good news of the Kingdom. Although we might fancy that Jesus selected individuals based upon their personal characteristics, it is equally plausible that he chose those among the twelve because of their capacity in working, their networks of relationships, their freedom of time in their work, and their ability to continue to receive support from their work. For example, Sean Freyne considers whether "the lifestyle of fishermen was more in tune with his own itinerant mode (Mt. 8.20; Lk. 9.58) than that of peasant farmers, tied to the land...."[5] Indeed, Jesus and his disciples often are depicted utilizing boats (Mark 3:7, 9; 4:1, 35–36; 5:18; 6:32, 45, 51; 8:10, etc.).

This raises another question, "Did Jesus distinguish some disciples from others, the worker-supporters from the apostle-missionaries?" After all, Jesus appointed the twelve to be with him and to send them out to preach the gospel and to cast out demons (Mark 3:13–15). Eventually, these twelve men would spread the gospel well beyond Judea. However, such a rigid distinction is not clearly supported in the Gospels. Followers of Jesus are not always called to leave their families and their work; Roman centurions presumably continued in their work (Matt 8:5–13; Acts 10) and Zaccheus and tax collectors stayed in their professions yet were reformed (Luke 7:29; 19:1–10). Even some who were enslaved as prostitutes and the property of others were welcomed by Jesus and enjoyed table fellowship with him.[6] Also, those obeying John the Baptist's call to repentance asked him how they should respond (Luke 3:10–14). John did not indicate that they should leave their jobs; rather, they should conduct themselves generously (sharing clothing and food), honestly, and not greedily (e.g., the soldier, the tax collectors). Yet, Jesus would seem to have pulled the twelve out of their jobs to spend intensive time with him relying presumably on the hospitality, homes, and resources of others.[7] Why? Was this the new and only model for the early church?

Here we need to understand that Jesus had specific missionary work for the twelve (Mark 9:7–13//Matt 10:5–23; Luke 9:1–10) and the seventy (Luke 10:1–22) before the imminent judgment that he foresaw coming upon the Jewish nation, i.e., the Jewish War with Rome in AD 70 that would take over one-million lives and result in more than a hundred-thousand souls taken into Roman slavery. He urged his followers to flee Judea during this calamity (Matt 24:16). In Luke 19:41–44, Jesus wept over the coming calamity of the Jewish War. Here in Luke's Gospel is the climax of Jesus's determination to travel to Jerusalem that began in 9:51. Jesus knew that he would die in Jerusalem where "all the prophets die" (13:33–34). Along this journey, when people wanted to be his followers, Jesus told one person that Jesus himself had no home; to another he said, "depart and announce the Kingdom of God," and to the last person, "No one, after putting his hand to the plow and looking backwards, is suited for the Kingdom of God" (9:57–62, my translations). Importantly, Jesus's "Missionary Discourse" in Matt 10 had its particular missional restriction to "the lost sheep of Israel" (Matt 10:5–6; cf. 15:24). Certainly, Jesus eventually commanded the apostles to make disciples beyond the land of Israel among all the nations, but only after his resurrection (Matt 28:19–20; Acts 1:8).

So, we must understand that Jesus's more immediate mission of the twelve apostles, who had left jobs presumably to rely on hospitality from village to village in Israel, was in view of his understanding of the imminent Jewish war (AD 70) that proved that Jesus was the Son of Man coming in his Kingdom (Matt 10:23; 16:27–28; 26:64). Jesus said, "you will not finish *going through* the cities of Israel until the Son of man comes" (Matt 10:23, emphasis mine). The same limitation is true of the seventy whom Jesus sent out ahead to villages as he travelled momentously to Jerusalem. Thus, the Kingdom's initial arrival in Jesus, the imminent judgment facing the nation of Israel, and the fall of its temple should not be confused (but very commonly is) with Jesus's final Parousia in his Second Coming (Matt 24:3, 27, 37, 39).

Taking a step back from these specifics, what this means is that Jesus's ministry plan of pulling apostles out of their paid professions or jobs was initially temporally conditioned by the constraints of the imminent Jewish war in Judea. Furthermore, if Jesus's followers were to extend this mission beyond the environs of Israel, other pragmatic constraints for mobility might apply, and indeed did. Work was often tied to a track of land or a centralized location and business site; to move outward required flexibility, but some jobs travel well. However, all jobs are valuable for God's Kingdom work, whether locally bound or free to spread abroad. As we will see in subsequent chapters, the church's historic adoption of full time paid ministers who work no other job does not reflect the complete picture of the spread of the first churches. Before looking at this, however, we need to consider Jesus's restoration of Peter and the disciples after his resurrection.

Peter's Restoration and the Business of the Church

As I indicated at the beginning of this chapter, we should question whether Jesus's first disciples failed by returning to their fishing work after his resurrection. Rather than suppose this, we should observer carefully what is recorded. Jesus actually helped them first to make a big catch and then proceeded to cook the fish and provided them a meal. In doing this, he was likely affirming them while also providing

an example for them to follow. As Craig S. Keener explains, "[M]ost
manual laborers seem to have taken pride in their work (they mention
their occupations on their tombstones); Jesus affirms their fishing, even
though that, too, had been his provision (21:5–6).... The risen Lord
has provided them more fish than they could possibly eat by
themselves."[8] Why so many fish? Why prepare the meal for them? At
this point in the episode, Jesus asked Peter famously three times
whether he loved him. We are so captivated by this that we often fail to
consider what Jesus commissions Peter to do in these three nearly
synonymous commands: "Feed [βόσκε] my lambs! ... Tend my sheep!
... Feed [βόσκε] my sheep!" (John 21:15–17 RSV). Who are these
lambs and sheep? Certainly, these refer to those for whom Jesus is
himself the Gate and the Shepherd (John 10:7–16; cf. Matt 9:36; cf.
10:6; 18:12).

However, what does it mean for Peter to "feed them"? The verb
"to feed" (βόσκω) only occurs nine times in the New Testament (twice
here in John) and elsewhere always referring to actual feeding (e.g.,
Matt 8:30; Luke 8:32; 15:15). But here in John, does the feeding refer
to providing physical sustenance or to something else, like teaching the
Word of God? Given the context of the miraculous catch of fish that
Jesus prepared for his disciples, we should understand the feeding to
include, if not even primarily entail, material provision. What John's
Gospel shows is Jesus's affirmation of work for the Kingdom (with
miraculous help occurring at times!) to help provide for the physical
needs of God's people, the vulnerable sheep (see John 6:1–14).

Jesus's command to Peter is consistent with the origins of Jesus's
use of the Shepherd/Sheep analogy—Ezekiel 34—where the shepherd
rulers of Israel failed to feed the flock, but engorged themselves (34:2–
3) and devoured their own sheep (34:10) at the expense of caring for
the needs, ailments, and lostness of the sheep (34:4–6). This
interpretation of Jesus's commands to Peter is also consistent with
Jesus's fulfilling Isaiah's Jubilee, proclaiming good news for the poor
and concern for their well-being as seen throughout especially Luke's
Gospel. So, in John 21 Jesus was restoring Peter for the work of the
Kingdom and calling him to use work and business to care for the
poor. This Kingdom work sounds very familiar with Spirit-led
entrepreneurial church planters in today's contexts.

Did Peter take this to heart and care for the sheep of God as
Jesus commanded him? Absolutely, in three ways. First, Peter

admonished leaders in the church to be shepherds of the sheep. As a fellow elder himself, Peter admonished the elders to "shepherd the flock ... not with dishonest gain but with goodwill, not lording over [κατακυριεύω] them, but becoming an example of the flock" (1 Pet 5:1–3). Implied here is material provision for those in need since Peter used the same term "lording over" that Jesus had used to critique the political leaders and benefactors (Matt 20:25//Mark 10:42//Luke 22:25 [κυριεύω]); at issue for Jesus, as for Peter, was the equitable use of resources without creating "dependency" and "subordination" of the socially-materially "lesser" persons on the powerful, wealthy "benefactors" who in the Roman system of patronage dispensed resources in order to receive praise while maintaining their positions of power and honor. In the Kingdom of God, the true Benefactor is God through his Regent-Broker Jesus Christ who models servanthood; any gift-giving and resource-sharing should be done without self-promotion or self-aggrandizement, but rather for God's glory in Christ. They have God to thank, and so should have no arrogant pride, but humbly serve.

Second, Peter encouraged all believers to grow in the faith (1 Pet 2:1–3), not to indulge in sinful desires and actions (1:14; 2:1, 11; 4:1–5, 15), but to be virtuous by being harmonious, sympathetic, humble, compassionate, and having brotherly love (3:8), to show evidence of good deeds (2:12; 3:11, 13, 16–17), to show love (4:8) and offer hospitality without complaint (4:9), to serve one another as good stewards of God's grace, and to speak and to serve for God's glory (4:11). Importantly, obedience to these admonitions would have involved the use of one's work, goods, and possessions to love, provide for, and offer hospitality to others, following the example of the elders (discussed above). Peter's exhortations reflect the teaching of Jesus. For example, "having compassion" in the Gospels involved proclamation of the gospel among the distressed and dispirited people (Matt 9:36), healing sickness/death/injury (Matt 14:14//Mark 6:34; Matt 20:34; Luke 7:13; 10:33), feeding the people (Matt 15:32//Mark 8:2; cf. Matt 14:14–16), and forgiving debts and sin (Matt 18:27; Luke 15:20). In 1 Peter 4:10–11 what Peter particularly stressed is "serving" (διακονέω) in response to God's gracious provision. This verb described the physical service offered to believers-in-need most essentially in matters of food (Luke 10:40; 12:37; 22:27; Acts 6:2, etc.), but also in sharing finances (Luke 8:3) and helping more broadly with thirst, hunger, clothing, visiting people in prison, and showing hospitality towards strangers (Matt 25:42–44; cf. Heb 6:10). In this regard, the apostle Paul's monetary collection, which I consider to be something like an international relief fund, was called a "serving" or "service" (διακονία; Rom 15:25, 31; 2 Cor 8:1–3, 19; cf. Acts 11:29–30).

Third and finally, Peter along with the apostles in Jerusalem were particularly interested in this collection for the poor. According to Paul's letter to the Galatians at 2:9–10 (written early around AD 48-49), the Jerusalem apostles accepted fellowship with him and simultaneously urged him to "remember the poor—the very thing I also was eager to do," said Paul. Bruce N. Longenecker has written extensively on *Remembering the Poor* as a focus of the early church that had its basis in the teaching of Jesus as well as Jewish life and ethical practice.[9] Indeed, in the next chapter we will explore how focal was "work" for the spread of the Gospel in Acts and in Paul while simultaneously providing for the poor and being generous to those in need. All such good work was facilitated by businesses. Compassion with capacity is a catalyst for ministry.

Conclusion

Focal in Jesus's proclamation in fulfilling Isaiah's Jubilee was freedom from debts/sins, proper valuation of human work, casting out demons, healing for the sick, and provision for the poor. If even many of his followers could not begin their own businesses and struggled with work in the unfair and lopsided economy of Israel that favored the those in power who lorded over the majority as their Benefactors, Jesus had shown his disciples the intersection of the gospel proclamation of the Kingdom, good work and business, and care for the poor. So, after Jesus's resurrection, Jesus restored Peter to feed the sheep. In Peter's admonitions to his flock, we see him bringing forward the teachings and practices of Jesus. Peter and his partner in spreading the Gospel, the apostle Paul, understood that the work of the Kingdom was to be conducted as service for the salvation and welfare of all people, especially those in the household of God (cf. Gal 6:10). In the next chapter, we will investigate the intersection of the marketplace with church planting in the book of Acts through ecclesial entrepreneurs like Paul.

---

[1] Jesus's question in 21:5, "Children, you don't have anything to eat, do you? (No.)" expects a negative answer and the disciples' "answer back" (ἀπεκρίθησαν from ἀποκρίνομαι) likely indicates their defensiveness. On the discourse function of ἀποκρίνομαι to indicate answering back or taking control in a challenge-riposte conversation, see Fredrick J. Long, *Koine Greek Grammar: A Beginning-Intermediate Exegetical and Pragmatic Handbook*, Accessible Greek Resources and Online Studies (Wilmore, KY: GlossaHouse, 2015), 356–58.

[2] See Issler, *Living into the Life of Jesus*, 190–91. He identifies seventeen parables. However, reviewing Jesus's parables, I have also included these other parables as involving business: Sower growing Seed (Mark 4:26–29), Placing Wine into proper Wineskins (Mark 2:21–22//Matt 9:17//Luke 5:37–39), the Prodigal Son, which involves work in foreign lands and restoration to the family's land (Luke 15:11–32), the Master and the Servant (Luke 17:7–10), the Pharisee and the Tax Collector (Luke 18:9–14), the Two Sons Working the Vineyard (Matt 21:28–32), the Great Banquet (Matt 22:1–14//Luke 14:16–24), and the Faithful Household Manager (Mark 13:34–37//Matt 24:42–51//Luke 12:35–48). Other parables that entail work processes, although no business may be necessarily implied, include, e.g., the parable of the woman placing leaven in dough (Matt 13:33–33//Luke 13:20–21). Stewardship of wealth, which implies business success, is found in the rich man and Lazarus (Luke 16:19–31) whereas stewardship of resources is seen in the parable of the Ten Virgins (Matt 25:1–13).

[3] This parable is difficult for interpreters. My summary has been informed by Craig S. Keener, *The IVP Bible Background Commentary: New Testament*, 1st ed. (Downers Grove, IL: InterVarsity, 1993), Luke 16:1–8.

[4] Klyne R. Snodgrass, "Parable," ed. Joel B. Green and Scot McKnight, *Dictionary of Jesus and the Gospels* (Downers Grove, IL: InterVarsity, 1992), 599.

[5] Sean Freyne, *Jesus, a Jewish Galilean: A New Reading of the Jesus Story* (London: T&T Clark, 2006), 52. Freyne is followed by Blake Wassell and Stephen Llewelyn, "'Fishers of Humans,' the Contemporary Theory of Metaphor, and Conceptual Blending Theory," *Journal of Biblical Literature* 133 (2014): 627–46 at 645.

[6] See the fascinating discussion in Mark Allan Powell, "Jesus and the Pathetic Wicked: Re-Visiting Sanders's View of Jesus' Friend-

ship with Sinners," *Journal for the Study of the Historical Jesus* 13.2–3 (2015): 188–208.

[7] See, e.g., Ben Witherington III, *The Gospel of Mark: A Socio-Rhetorical Commentary* (Grand Rapids: Eerdmans, 2001), 421–22. He says, "Jesus seems to take up residence, possibly, in Simon's house in Capernaum or to have used it as a base for operations early on (cf. 1:29; 2:1). In any case, he makes himself at home where his first disciples live." Although I cannot find direct evidence of this, it seems possible to me that the first apostles may have been funded from their former (family) businesses; e.g., the apostles have some means to pay for food for the poor (Luke 9:13//Mark 6:37) and Peter to maintain a household residence.

[8] Keener, *IVP Bible Background Commentary: New Testament,* comment on John 21:9–10 and 21:11.

[9] Bruce W. Longenecker, *Remember the Poor: Paul, Poverty, and the Greco-Roman World* (Grand Rapids: Eerdmans, 2010); Bruce W. Longenecker and Kelly D. Liebengood, eds., *Engaging Economics: New Testament Scenarios and Early Christian Reception,* 1st ed. (Grand Rapids: Eerdmans, 2009).

CHAPTER 5

Ecclesial Entrepreneurs in Acts and Paul

Fredrick J. Long

Introduction

With the foundation of Jesus's teaching and his embodiment of the in-breaking Kingdom of God, Peter and the disciples advanced their understanding of the good news by proclaiming the Word and sharing resources with one another (Acts 2:44–45). In so doing, they brought forward Jesus's kingdom work with the spread of God's Word. Looking at the Book of Acts and the apostle Paul in this chapter, we will see how this new wine of Jesus found fresh entrepreneurial models in the growth of the first churches. Once again, I will structure this essay by first addressing problematic Myths that need adjustment, if not even correction, in our understanding.

1. Myth 1: *Acts is simply about the growth of the early Church and the spread of the Word of God, not business models.* However, the preface of Acts introducing the book most closely resembles prefaces used in ancient trade or professional manuals.[1] Moreover, notably Acts often highlights ancient occupations and places of work showing how the spread of the Gospel encourages networking among businesses, transforms those places of work with the truth of the Gospel, and confronts illegitimate work. There is much here to consider for church growth and entrepreneurial church planting today.

2. <u>Myth 2</u>: *Paul's tentmaking work is an exception for church planting, not the rule, since Paul established clearly distinct ministerial positions or offices (elders and deacons) in his letters who should receive pay for their work (1 Tim 5:17–18; 1 Cor 9:14; cf. Luke 10:7).* While it is true that there is a place to pay ministers of the Gospel (perhaps even a primary place), it is not at all clear that all ministers in the New Testament were paid, nor less clear even that they did not work other jobs while ministering. Moreover, the New Testament exhibits Paul's approach as an alternative church planting model: Paul himself refused to be paid and worked rather with his own hands for several reasons: his particular calling, the social setting of the broader Mediterranean world, and his desire for believers to imitate him.

3. <u>Myth 3</u>: *Business and the church do not mix in Paul.* Not true. In fact, Paul's description of the characteristics of ministers in the Pastoral Epistles drew upon contemporaneous "business manuals" that described best practices for household management. This has implications for how valuable our own modern, contemporaneous business models may be for the church as long as the truth of the Gospel in imitation of Christ is kept central. To the extent that the church reflects "best business ethics and practice," it witnesses to the truth, goodness, and transformative power of the Gospel.

4. <u>Myth 4</u>: *Human effort or "works" are attempts to earn our salvation according to Paul; moreover, earning money profits us nothing in this world. We must remember Paul's statement, "The love of money is the root of all evils" (1 Tim 6:10).* However, it is undeniable that Paul called followers of Christ to do good (Rom 12:2, 9, 21; 13:3–4; 15:2, 14; 16:19, etc.) and to walk in "good deeds" (Eph 2:10; Titus 2:7, 14; 3:8, etc.); in fact, our actions of doing good or not will be judged in the Gospel (Rom 2:6–10; cf. Matt 16:27). So, while we are seeking to do good, we also conduct our work such that we do not love money more than God and God's good news; instead, we are called to do good in the work of our business for the sake of the Gospel.

Spreading the Gospel in Occupations to Save and to Serve Those in Need

What kind of literature is the Book of Acts? Although scholars have debated this recently—history, biography, biographical history, even fiction—not sufficiently appreciated is how the preface of Acts 1:1–11 orients its audiences to its material content. Building on Loveday Alexander's research, Vernon K. Robbins indicates that the preface in Acts is most analogous with "profession-oriented writings."

> This literature is written by and for networks of people in "the world of the crafts and professions" in Mediterranean society: artisans, tradesmen, businessmen, businesswomen, physicians, engineers—people at the level of the professions and guilds— rather than networks of people in the literary circles of Mediterranean society.... [I]t is writing for networks of people who exchange goods and services with one another regularly because they share a belief that Jesus of Nazareth and his followers are continuing the history of Israel.[2]

The implications of this are far reaching: Luke's understanding of Jesus's fulfilling Scripture and the Jubilee vision of Isaiah is extended throughout the Book of Acts as the early church conducts the fruitful labor of proclamation and occupation for the Kingdom. Rather than replacing businesses with the proclamation of the Gospel, the work of spreading the good news comes alongside and infiltrates human occupations. This is seen throughout Acts in pivotal ways.

On the one hand, many places of business become places of witness, re-purposed spaces of worship, and resources of networking. Primary here are homes where businesses commonly were housed. In Acts, houses in various cities become places of proclamation, worship, fellowship, healing, and hospitality: the upper room (1:13; 2:2), the "breaking of bread from house to house" (2:46), "teaching and preaching from house to house" (5:42), the house of Judas in Damascus (9:11–19), the upper room of Tabitha's house in Joppa (9:36–42), Simon the Tanner's house there (9:43; 10:32), the centurion Cornelius's house in Caesarea (ch.10, reported again in ch.11), Mary's house (the mother of John Mark) in Jerusalem (12:12–19), Lydia's household at Philippi (16:14–15, 40), the home of Jason at Thessalonica (17:1-9), the house of co-tentmakers Aquila and Priscilla at Corinth (18:1–3), the upper room at Troas (20:6–11), "teaching from house to house" (20:20), and the house of Philip at Caesarea (21:8–10). Although we don't know to what extent these homes were centers of business, many are explicitly connected to businesses; also, every home was indebted to business (somewhere) in their capacity to host (room and board) church members. Additionally, Acts specifies other occupational places by name where God in Christ breaks in: the prison at Philippi (16:23–35), the market place at Athens (17:17), the intellectual center Areopagus at Athens (17:19–34), the lecture hall of Tyrannus in Ephesus (19:9–10), the residence of Publius, the leading man on the island of Malta (28:7–10), the Market of Appius and the Three Inns of Rome (28:15), the soldier's apartment in Rome (28:16, 23), and Paul's rented quarters there (28:30). God also assisted the sailing venture that carried the prisoner Paul on board speaking through him, but the captain's failure to heed led to "damage and loss" (Paul's wording) although Paul continued to encourage them to take right actions in order to save their souls (Acts 27:6, 9–12, 21–26, 31–36, 44). Paul was concerned for the goods and their souls, mirroring God's concern. Thus, Acts shows the spread of the gospel through places of business; God is not anti-business, but pro-business in the proclamation of the gospel.

On the other hand, some occupations are threatened if not even invalidated. Magic and its profits are confronted and exposed (Simon Magus in 8:9–24; the sons of Sceva in 19:13–16; the burning of expensive scrolls in 19:18–19). Profit from fortune-telling through divination is thwarted and the slave woman is freed from the spirit possessing her (16:16–21). The prosperous idol-making business in Ephesus (and everywhere implied) is undermined (19:24–41). Thus, the Gospel as it spreads reveals that God is working through people's work while exposing dubious, harmful, and idolatrous work in which dark forces of evil are at play. Ultimately, the good news redeems and liberates human souls from corruption, fraud, and deception for fruitful work and service in the Kingdom of God.

Why is productive service needed? The Book of Acts shows the earliest believers organizing and sharing their resources to facilitate ministry and to help those in need (Acts 2:44–45; 4:32), especially the widows (6:1–7). Special care for the widows is attested furthermore in 1 Tim 5:1–16 and James 1:27. What made such help possible were the resources given to those leading the churches, for example, the apostles in Jerusalem (Acts 4:34–37). However, the revenue was also raised through members in the church working businesses. For example, in the town of Joppa the female disciple Tabitha (named also Dorcas) was known for "deeds of kindness and charity which she continually did" (Acts 9:36). Women could work businesses. Craig S. Keener summarizes, "[i]n one analysis of Roman funerary inscriptions (relevant for Roman Corinth), although women were absent in construction, banking, and transportation, they constituted 47 percent of skilled service, 27 percent of domestic service, 15 percent of those involved in manufacturing, 8 percent of sales, and 3 percent of those involved in administration."[3] Tabitha made and gave clothing to the widows living there (also with her?) who showed their garments to Peter when he had been called in to pray over Tabitha who had recently died (9:39). Peter prayed and presented her alive to the saints and widows there (9:40–42). Significantly, Peter stayed in Joppa for many days enjoying the hospitality of Simon who is identified as a "tanner [of leather]" (9:43). Interestingly, it is significant that this same chapter (Acts 9), which shows repeatedly the intersection of gospel outreach with businesses and their locations, *also introduces the apostle Paul's conversion.* Paul was an innovator who embodied a new entrepreneurial model of "tentmaking" in the ministry of the Gospel.

The Apostle Paul's Tentmaking

Paul was an "apostolic innovator" as described by T. Michael W. Halcomb in his important study of *Paul the Change Agent: The Context, Aims, and Implications of an Apostolic Innovator.*[4] In God's wisdom, Paul was raised up and on the basis of God's calling he decided not to receive payment for preaching the gospel but rather to work with his own hands in a tentmaking occupation (1 Cor 4:12; 9:1–18; 2 Cor 6:5; 11:23, 27; 1 Thess 2:9; 2 Thess 3:8; Acts 18:3; 20:34–35). This is significant, as Halcomb explains, because

> Paul often lifted himself up as an example for the congregants to follow and imitate…. [T]he apostle's mimetic appeals are calls to both imitate his change as well as his role as a change agent…. As a change agent, Paul's innovation was the gospel. He preached and taught the gospel in congregations that can be described as having a centralized diffusion system. He employed a rhetoric of change in each epistle and used strategies within his change agent repertoire to meet the needs of the recipients of his letters in his various congregations.[5]

Paul's willingness to change the paradigm came at some cost and misunderstanding to him as is attested in 1 and 2 Corinthians (see esp.

1 Cor 4:10–12; 2 Cor 11:27). Manual labor was not viewed positively by all people in Roman society, as is the case more generally today. Yet, Paul repeatedly called followers of Christ to imitate him (1 Thess 1:6; 2 Thess 3:7–9; 1 Cor 4:16; 11:1; Phil 3:17; 4:9) which probably involved also the notion of "working" just as Paul purposefully exemplified for converts (1 Thess 2:9; 2 Thess 3:7–9) and commanded of them (1 Thess 4:11; 2 Thess 3:10–13; Eph 4:28).

But, what was Paul's profession? Actually, we do not know exactly. In Acts 18:3 we learn that Paul with Aquila and Priscilla were "tentmakers by trade" (σκηνοποιοὶ τῇ τέχνῃ). The word σκηνοποιός "tentmaker" occurs only here in Scripture and two other places in all available ancient Greek writing. There were different types of tents and materials used to make them (leather or fabric). Most likely, the tents were made of leather of some kind (for instance, military tents, business awnings, tents in the forum, theater tents, etc.). Alternatively, another view in non-scholarly sources (as far as I could find) maintains that Paul made private Jewish "prayer tents." Regardless of the exact occupation, Paul utilized his transportable work to support himself, to network among his peers (believers and non-believers alike), and to supply the needs of others. Paul's work affected his comings and goings not unlike other Jewish merchants of his day (see James 4:11–13); they depended on commercial shipping routes while also networking with others in the same trade who tended to congregate together in districts within cities sometimes even with roads named after their profession.[6] The spirit among those working the same trade was more cooperative than competitive. Keener more recently provides a very helpful survey of the context of ancient work, business, and Paul's tentmaking.[7] Also, the study on his tentmaking by Ronald F. Hock is still worth reading to understand the circumstances of ancient guilds and networking.[8]

Why did Paul work while proclaiming the gospel and what implication does this have for us today? These are important and complex questions. From 1 Thess 2:1–13, it would seem that Paul wanted to distance himself from any possible motive of deceit or chicanery, such as was common among travelling sophists of his day who wanted to get paid for their speaking/teaching as a form of entertainment but without lasting value.[9] Also, Paul does not appear to receive payment from those he was directly and immediately ministering to. This was probably to avoid a conflict among those who might compete to patronize him and to prevent any loss of his freedom or integrity since, as one receiving financial support, he was socially obligated to show partiality to his patron. In fact, refusing the patronage of the (wealthy) Corinthian believers amounted to a snub on Paul's part against them and led to enmity that Paul must address in his letters to them.[10] Money/tithes/gifts given for ministers often comes from the wealthiest who then too often expect to have the loudest voice and influence on the minister. This sort of "patronage" is what Paul opposed with the Corinthians and in his ministry in general. As a result, Paul appears only to have accepted financial assistance from a church *while he was ministering in another location so that the givers did not receive "direct" benefit or even honor/praise (rightly belonging to God alone) for their generous giving to him.* For instance, when he received help from the Philippian church (the Macedonians of 2 Cor 8:1–5), it was while he was in need at Ephesus. The Letter of Philippians asks for further assistance while he was in need at Rome. This practice encouraged believers to be generous to others without immediate reciprocal repayment, thus allowing them to see themselves as "ministering/serving" (the Greek verb διακονέω) in God's work, and not for their own praise and honor, which was the norm in the Greco-Roman patronage system. This also explains why Paul's international relief fund (the collection effort) is repeatedly described precisely as "ministering/serving" (2 Cor 9:1–5, 12–15).

In contemporary contexts, too, I have often perceived this problem: Church attendees pay ministers for doing ministry and then assume that they don't need to do ministry or aren't qualified for church ministry. This is hugely problematic. Also, I have seen smaller churches struggle to pay for their minister's salary, and this becomes burdensome to both the pastor and the parishioners, sometimes leading to that church closing. Finally, pastors are sometimes perceived as not being hard working, whether true or not; Paul strongly resisted this perception and rather set himself up as an example of earnest labor, working long hours (Acts 20:31, 35; 1 Thess 2:9; 2 Thess 3:8). It is intriguing to consider that adopting a tentmaking approach to planting churches may help maintain the integrity of ministry by actually requiring the leaders of the church to adopt values, skills, practices, and virtues that are integral to running a business well. In fact, the Apostle Paul described church leadership within "the household of God" precisely by drawing upon ancient discussions that discussed best household management virtues.

Virtues of Church Leadership
and Contemporary Business Models

Paul's description of the characteristics of ministers in the Pastoral Epistles borrows from contemporaneous "business manuals" that discussed best practices for household management conducted by stewards (many times slaves) who oversaw the business and management of the property. Indeed, for Paul "the proper conduct in the household of God" is at stake (1 Tim 3:15; cf. 1 Tim 1:4). Stressed here is that the church as household belongs to God and is under God's jurisdiction. This astounding connection was described initially by Edwin Hatch,[11] and has been recently re-discovered in scholarship.[12] Although Paul thinks here metaphorically at some level (THE HOUSEHOLD OF GOD IS LIKE A HUMAN HOUSEHOLD and should be managed analogously), still the extensive degree of correspondence would suggest that in Paul's mind an integral relationship between business at home and in the church assembly existed.[13]

Because of the importance of these attributes for the office of overseer in 1 Tim 3:1-7, I include the NASB translation along with some notes on important Greek word definitions.[14]

"An overseer, then, must be…"

1. **above reproach** [ἀνεπίλημπτος, ον (also ἀνεπίληπτος) strictly, *not to be laid hold of;* hence, of moral conduct *blameless, above criticism, without fault* (1 Tim 5:7).],
2. **the husband of one wife** [μιᾶς γυναικὸς ἄνδρα],
3. **temperate** [νηφάλιος, ία, ον strictly, *holding no wine, without wine;* of persons, *sober, temperate, abstinent*],
4. **prudent** [σώφρων, ον gen. ονος strictly, *having a sound or healthy mind;* as having ability to curb desires and impulses so as to produce a measured and orderly life *self-controlled, sensible*],
5. **respectable** [κόσμιος, ον strictly, *well arranged;* (1) of persons, *disciplined, honorable, respectable* (1 Tim 3:2); (2) of dress characterized by respectability *modest, sensible* (1 Tim 2:9)],
6. **hospitable** [φιλόξενος, ον strictly, *stranger loving;* hence, *hospitable, kind to strangers* (1 Pet 4:9)],
7. **able to teach,** [διδακτικός, ή, όν *skillful in teaching, able to teach* (1 Tim 3:2)]

8. **not addicted to wine** [πάροινος, ον *addicted to wine, drunken,* of one who tends to be quarrelsome as he habitually drinks too much; as a noun, *drunkard*]

9. **nor pugnacious** [πλήκτης, ου, ὁ strictly, *a striker;* hence, *a pugnacious person, bully, quarrelsome person.*]

10. but **gentle** [ἐπιεικής, ές *gentle, kind, forbearing* (1 Tim 3:3); substantive (as a noun) τὸ ἐπιεικές equivalent to ἡ ἐπιείκεια *gentleness, forbearance* (Phil 4:5)],

11. **peaceable** [ἄμαχος, ον *not disposed to fight* or *quarrel, peaceable.*],

12. **free from the love of money**.

13. *He must be* **one who manages [προΐστημι] his own household well**,   [προΐστημι only intransitive in the New Testament (1) middle voice *put oneself (responsibly) at the head, lead, direct, rule* (1 Tim 5:17); (2) active, of a protective leadership *care for, help, give aid* (1 Thess 5:12); (3) of responsible preoccupation with something *devote oneself to, engage in, strive for* (Titus 3:8). See Rom 12:8; 1 Thess 5:12; 1 Tim 3:12; 5:17.]

    a. **keeping his children under control [ἐν ὑποταγῇ] with all dignity [μετὰ πάσης σεμνότητος]** [ὑποταγή, ῆς, ἡ only passive voice in the New Testament *submission, obedience, subjection.*] [σεμνότης, τητος, ἡ as serious and worthy conduct which earns reverence and respect *dignity, seriousness, propriety.*]

    b. **"but if a man does not know how to manage his own household, how will he take care of the church of God?"**

14. *and* **not a new convert** [νεόφυτον], [*purpose*] **so that he will not become conceited** [τυφωθεὶς] [*cause*] **and fall into the condemnation** [effect] **incurred by the devil.** [shared fate] [τυφόω (1) lit. *wrap in smoke* or *mist, becloud;* (2) only figurative and passive voice in the New Testament (a) *be puffed up, be very proud* or *arrogant* (1 Tim 3:6); (b) *be silly, stupid, absurd* from a sense of one's own importance (2 Tim 3:4).]

15. **And he must have a good reputation** [μαρτυρίαν καλὴν] **with those outside** *the church,* [*purpose*] **so that he will not fall into reproach** [*ill-repute; disgrace*] **and the snare** [παγίδα] **of the devil**. [παγίς, ίδος, ἡ (1) lit. anything which catches and holds fast *snare, trap, noose, net* (Luke 21:35); (2)

metaphoric (a) used in Rom 11:9 of a false sense of security which leads to a sudden and unexpected judgment *pitfall, concealed danger, source of error;* (b) as a stratagem of the devil for gaining control *deceitful trick, entanglement* (1 Tim 3:7); (3) figurative as any allurement to wrongdoing *enticement, temptation, attraction* (1 Tim 6:9).]

That Paul would use contemporary thinking on best business virtues for household management has implications for how we might discerningly glean insights from our own best contemporaneous business models today in our respective cultural settings. Although not an entirely one-to-one correspondence, the virtuous character, the appropriate professionalism, the efficient management, and the wise structuring of the church as like a business household would have testified to unbelievers of the truth of the Gospel; it can also do so today. The Apostle Paul was painfully aware that unbelievers would be observing the church (e.g., 1 Cor 14:16, 23–25). In 1 Tim 2 he urged believers to be good and show virtuous conduct for all to see since "God wants all people to be saved" (2:4).[15] Thus, when onlookers would have viewed the interconnected life of church members, they would not have seen something foreign and out of the order, but something familiar, well-managed, and productive. This would have testified to them. Sadly, today some churches are perceived and portrayed as exclusive social-clubs, or worse, as irrelevant, obscure cabals that are disconnected from meaningful life and social discourse.

Did the early church pay its ministers? It is not at all clear that they were paid; according to 1 Tim 5:17–18, perhaps only those who preached and taught. Moreover, it is not clear whether even these worked additional jobs for pay. Full payment to ministers may have been restricted to two categories of people: 1) "frontline" missionaries who invested all of their time preaching in new locations where no local support from businesses had yet been established; and 2) those who dedicated themselves to preaching and teaching. Why would this latter group be paid? Anyone who has studied Scripture—and I mean, really studied Scripture diligently accessing the original languages and searching the whole counsel of God's Word—and prepared material to teach knows that such work takes considerable time to do well; it is a full-time job. This would have been even more so given the daylight and working constraints in a pre-industrial, pre-computer, pre-internet environment. Also, there was a well-established tradition in Greco-Roman culture to pay stable, reputable teachers, whereas travelling sophists looking for a quick buck were suspect. Significantly, Paul urged paying those who taught and preached: "The one who is taught the word is to share all good things with the one who teaches" (Gal 6:6 NASB). At the same time, Paul called on followers of Christ to do good to all people, especially for those in the household of God (Gal 6:10).

Good Works in Paul

Although Paul stated clearly that we are unable to save ourselves, at the same time he called believers to "redeem the time" (Eph 5:16)—literally, "buy up opportunities," a metaphor from the marketplace—and to "be fruitful doing deeds of righteousness" (5:9–10). In response to God's grace through Jesus's good work and sacrifice, Paul indicated that believers were to "walk in good deeds" (2:8–10). This productive "work" is God-given and predicated upon God's "good" work in creation (Gen 2:2–3, 15, 18). Paul repeatedly expressed to believers that working for resources afforded them the opportunity to earn something in order to give to those in need (Eph 4:28; 1 Thess 4:11; 2 Thess 3:8, 11–13; 2 Cor 9:6–12; Rom 15:26–27; Titus 3:8, 14; cf. Luke 3:11). If care for the poor and needy required resources, then believers ought to be concerned to work for wealth in order to give.

One of my doctoral students, Luke Thomas Post, is researching and writing his dissertation on references to the "good" in Paul's writings.[16] It is truly fascinating research and the eventual publication of it will bless the church. What Luke has shown thus far is that Paul's admonition to do good shows up as a generalizing command near the end in his earliest letters (Gal 6:6–10; 1 Thess 5:15, 21; 2 Thess 3:13). From the context of these writings in addition to Ephesians, such good is produced from "work" to provide benefit for others (1 Thess 2:9; 4:11–12; 2 Thess 3:6–15; Eph 4:28). Importantly, Paul's admonition of believers to do the good in 2 Thess 2:15–17 is in view of the "traditions" that they had received in word or in letter (cf. 2 Thess 3:6; 1 Cor 11:2, 23). This word "tradition" likely referred to teaching material that originated with Jesus himself and had been passed along by the first disciples through Paul. Similarly, Paul's command to work with one's hands and to do good to share with one having a need (Eph 4:28) follows upon his prior urging believers to learn Christ and to be taught the truth "in Jesus" (4:20–21), referring to the earthly, historical Jesus as he lived as a human being embodying the message of God's Kingdom come. Thus, Paul's writings show continuity with Jesus in the manner of the work of good deeds for the good of others in the context of the proclamation of the good news of the Gospel. Paul understood that God's redemption of humans restores them to productive, fruitful living to bless others.

Conclusion

Although earnings from business and work may be assumed in the Book of Acts, Luke endeavored to show how the Gospel spread through homes and across various business sectors. One benefit of adopting a business model for the church assembly is that its centralizing location provided a place to meet and worship. The early house churches reflected this benefit. Additionally, the Book of Acts shows how the growth of the early Church occurred within the environment of a variety of other workspaces; the good news is not anti-business, but pro-business. At the same time, the work of the Gospel challenged illegitimate income and businesses that would deceive and enslave people. Also featured in the Book of Acts is the Apostle Paul who was an apostolic innovator. He revealed another ministry model, one of working with his own hands as he ministered to people. Such mobile work freed him up to preach the gospel without any strings attached. However, more than this, Paul offered himself as an example for believers to follow who would be able to work themselves in order to give to those in need.

In the end, the intersection of the Gospel and business is a natural one since this is found in Jesus as well as God's design for his good creation. In Christ, God uses the locus of the church assembly and household for humans and their work to be redeemed. This is good news for entrepreneurial church planters who look to Jesus, the earliest disciples, and Paul for examples to emulate. The next chapter will explore how the call for entrepreneurial church planting is in fact rooted in the Great Commission of Jesus.

[1] Loveday Alexander, "Luke's Preface in the Context of Greek Preface-Writing," *Novum Testamentum* 28.1 (1986): 48–74 at 57.

[2] Vernon K. Robbins, "The Claims of the Prologues and Greco-Roman Rhetoric: The Prefaces to Luke and Acts in Light of Greco-Roman Rhetorical Strategies," in *Jesus and the Heritage of Israel: Luke's Narrative Claim Upon Israel's Legacy*, ed. David P. Moessner (Harrisburg, PA: Trinity Press International, 1999), 63–83 at 66. Robbins does not elaborate on this insight in the essay, but instead describes in detail the prologues of Luke and Acts in view of the rhetorical progymnasmata exercises.

[3] Craig S. Keener, *Acts: An Exegetical Commentary*, 4 vols. (Grand Rapids: Baker Academic, 2012), 2714.

[4] T. Michael W. Halcomb, *Paul the Change Agent: The Context, Aims, and Implications of an Apostolic Innovator*, GlossaHouse Dissertation Series 2 (Wilmore, KY: GlossaHouse, 2015).

[5] Halcomb, *Paul the Change Agent*, 215–16.

[6] See, e.g., Edward B. Pollard, "Commerce," ed. James Orr et al., *The International Standard Bible Encyclopaedia* (Chicago: The Howard-Severance Company, 1915), 688. So also Keener: "That Paul would find fellow Jews of the same trade is no more surprising than his ministry starting in the synagogues" (*Acts*, 2719).

[7] Keener, *Acts*, 2714–2736.

[8] Ronald F. Hock, *Social Context of Paul's Ministry: Tent-Making and Apostleship* (Philadelphia: Augsburg Fortress, 1980).

[9] The classic study on this is by Bruce W. Winter, "The Entries and Ethics of Orators and Paul (1 Thessalonians 2:1–12)," *Tyndale Bulletin* 44.1 (1993): 55–74.

[10] See the profound study of Peter Marshall, *Enmity in Corinth: Social Conventions in Paul's Relations with the Corinthians*, WUNT 2.23 (Tübingen: Mohr Siebeck, 1987). On 2 Corinthians, see my technical study of the charges level against Paul that included his failed travel plans, inconsistency of his word, and financial trickery in handling money; Fredrick J. Long, *Ancient Rhetoric and Paul's Apology: The Compositional Unity of 2 Corinthians*, SNTSMS 131 (Cambridge: Cambridge University Press, 2004).

[11] Edwin Hatch, *The Organization of the Early Christian Churches. Eight Lectures Delivered Before the University of Oxford, in the Year 1880, on the*

Foundation of the Late Rev. John Bampton, 3rd ed. (London: Longmans, Green, & Co., 1918).

¹² See Abraham J. Malherbe, "Overseers as Household Managers in the Pastoral Epistles," in *Text, Image, and Christians in the Graeco-Roman World a Festschrift in Honor of David Lee Balch*, ed. Aliou Cissé Niang and Carolyn A. Osiek, Princeton Theological Monograph Series 176 (Eugene, OR: Pickwick, 2012), 72–88 and John K. Goodrich, "Managing God's Household: Overseers as Stewards and the Qualifications for Leadership in the Pastoral Epistles," in *Disputed Pauline Section* (paper presented at the Society of Biblical Literature Annual Conference, San Francisco, November 21, 2011); idem, "Overseers as Stewards and the Qualifications for Leadership in the Pastoral Epistles," *Zeitschrift für die Neutestamentliche Wissenschaft und Kunde der Älteren Kirche* 104 (2013): 77–97.

¹³ See especially Goodrich, "Managing God's Household."

¹⁴ Greek word definitions and data (slightly modified) are from Barbara and Timothy Friberg, *Analytical Lexicon of the Greek New Testament*, Baker's Greek New Testament Library 4 (Grand Rapids: Baker, 2000), s.v.

¹⁵ For a survey of the extensive appeal to social decorum and virtuous behavior for evangelistic effect in 1 Tim 2, see my article "A Wife in Relation to a Husband: Greek Discourse Pragmatic and Cultural Evidence for Interpreting 1 Tim 2:11–15," *The Journal of Inductive Biblical Studies* 2.2 (2015): 6–43 available at http://place.asburyseminary.edu/jibs/vol2/iss2/3/.

¹⁶ Luke will probably defend his dissertation in the spring of 2019, and I have his permission to refer here briefly to his work.

Great Commission: Theological Foundations and Implications for Marketplace Ministry

Timothy C. Tennent

Introduction

The picture of the followers of Jesus being scattered like seed into the world is one of the most enduring metaphors of the people of God. The growing professionalization of ministry and the credentialing gatekeeping that surrounds the ordination process has almost eclipsed the natural ministry of Christians in the workplace. It is the purpose of this chapter to explore the final commission of Jesus Christ to his Church and set it within the larger frame of the *missio dei* that calls all of God's people for witness and ministry in the world. I will do this by exploring each of the "Great Commission" passages in the New Testament.

Clarifications Concerning the "Great Commission(s)"

The common phrase "Great Commission" is a relatively late expression used to refer to the final commission of Jesus Christ to his disciples. For example, William Carey, widely regarded as the father of the modern missionary movement, never uses the phrase "Great Commission" in his landmark treatise known as *An Enquiry*. Its first appearance in print seems to be in the three-volume *History of the*

Church Mission Society published in 1899.[1] The phrase is often identified specifically with Matthew 28:18–20 and, unfortunately, is frequently treated as an isolated pericope, separated from the rest of the gospel as well as the larger biblical context. It is beyond the scope of this study to fully explore the history of the interpretation of 28:18–20 in church history. However, suffice it to say, there is ample evidence to demonstrate that through much of church history it was not generally quoted as a missionary text because it was thought to have already been fulfilled by the original Apostles who received the commission. The text was largely used for other purposes, and its full import was often obscured by ecclesiastical controversies. A survey of its usage shows that it is far more likely to be cited as a text in support for the deity of Christ, the Trinity, or the precise language to be used in baptismal formulas, than as the basis for any missionary mandate.[2]

The relatively scant treatment of this text as the basis for missions is to be contrasted with the modern period where it is quoted regularly and is the subject of countless books and articles. Today, it is common to encounter this final commission of Christ being referred to in the most exalted terms, including phrases such as the "Great Commission," the "final Manifesto," the "climax" of Jesus's ministry, or "the most important concern of the gospel."[3] While the spotlight on this particular text has, on the whole, benefited the church, it has also caused misunderstandings about the nature of the missionary mandate to the church and how it is connected to the *missio dei*. It has also tended to isolate these particular texts from their natural connection to the gospels out of which they come. Therefore, it is important that several clarifications be made at the outset of this chapter.

The "Great Commission" Refers to Multiple Texts, not a Single Text

First, the phrase "Great Commission" is used to designate an *entire range of texts* found in the New Testament, not simply the well-known passage found in Matthew 28:18–20. Each of the gospels, as well as the book of Acts, records a dramatic pericope of commissioning to a group of gathered disciples. These texts are found in Matthew 28:18–20, Mark 16:14–18, Luke 24:44–49, John 20:19–23, and Acts 1:7–8.

Second, it is important to remember that these passages are all post-resurrection sayings of Christ given at various times and places.

The fact that these passages are all uttered by the Risen Lord is, in itself, sufficient reason to refer to these commissions with the adjective "great," especially given the narrow forty-day time frame, and how little is generally recorded of the post-resurrection discourses of Jesus.

The descriptor "great" gains even further credibility when we recognize how central it was to the teaching of Christ during the post-resurrection period. It is not unusual for single events, miracles or sayings of Christ to be commonly recorded in the synoptic gospels and, occasionally, in all four. However, this does not seem to be the case with the final commissions of Jesus Christ to his disciples. Not only is the language between the accounts remarkably distinct, but also they are set in diverse settings. This means that Jesus repeats various versions of the Great Commission in various places over a forty-day period, including Galilee, Jerusalem, in a closed and locked room the night of the resurrection, and just prior to the Ascension in Bethany.

Third, the particularity of these various commissioning discourses demand that each be explored within the integrity and larger context of its own biblical setting. The gospel writers all place these commissioning texts in a position which serves as a climax to the gospel story they are unfolding. These texts are impoverished when they are taken out of that context and interpreted in isolation. The challenge is to make certain that each text is allowed to speak in its own distinctive voice, while, at the same time, seeing how they collectively serve the church and connect in their own way with the larger *missio dei*. The next section of this chapter will seek to examine each of the texts within the larger frame to which they belong.

Matthew: Fulfilling the Abrahamic Promise by Making Disciples of all Nations

Matthew's Gospel and the Mission to "All Nations"

We must begin by demonstrating how Matthew 28:18–20 fits within the larger context of Matthew's gospel. Some representative texts in Matthew's gospel will demonstrate that the final commission is fully consistent with, and flows out of, the larger message of the gospel.

1. Genealogy. Only Matthew and Luke contain genealogies of Jesus. Matthew's genealogy is unique in that it includes four Gentile women: Tamar (1:3), Rahab (1:5), Ruth (1:5), and Bathsheba (1:6), whereas Luke's genealogy contains no mention of any women, or of

Gentiles. Tamar and Rahab are Canaanites, Ruth is a Moabite and Bathsheba is widely believed to be a Hittite. The inclusion of these names serves to remind Matthew's Jewish readers that there are faithful, godly people who are part of the Gentile nations of the world and that God's transformative grace extends to all nations.

2. <u>Magi</u>. The journey of the Gentile magi from the east coming to offer gifts of gold, frankincense and myrrh to Jesus is a powerful symbol of the nations of the world streaming to the Jewish messiah. Their presence in the opening pages of Matthew's gospel recalls the prophecy of Isaiah that "nations will come to your light, kings to the brightness of your dawn" (Isaiah 60:3).[4] Matthew frames his entire gospel by the nations streaming to Jesus (magi) at the beginning, and the disciples streaming out to the nations (Great Commission) at the end. It should also be noted that these gifts being brought to Jesus are derived from the marketplace and thus, both prophecy and fulfillment are reminders that the whole of human commerce falls under the sovereignty of Jesus Christ.

3. <u>Fleeing to Egypt</u>. Immediately following the visit of the Magi, Matthew records the relocation of Joseph, Mary and Jesus to Egypt (2:13–15). This is, of course, significant as Jesus re-enacts the Exodus whereby the children of Israel came up out of Egypt (Hosea 11:1). However, it should not be overlooked that this also represents "the transformation of Egypt from a symbol of oppression and bondage (Deut 5:5 & 15) to a haven and protector of Israel's messiah."[5] It is a refreshing testimony to the power of the gospel to reconcile nations.

4. <u>Inauguration of Jesus's Ministry</u>. In Matthew's gospel, Jesus begins his ministry in "Galilee of the Gentiles" and later, at the conclusion of his gospel, Matthew alone records Jesus and the angels directing the disciples back to Galilee (26:32; 28:7) in order to receive the final commission to "all nations" (28:18–20). In Matthew's gospel Jesus begins and ends his life and ministry "on the field," symbolized by Egypt and Galilee, not Jerusalem, the center of Judaism, of revelation and the Temple.

5. <u>God's Grace beyond Israel in Matthew's Gospel</u>. Matthew includes a wide selection of Christ's teachings that are quite explicit in demonstrating that Israel has no automatic claim to the Kingdom, over against the unbelieving Gentiles. In the Parable of the Workers in the Vineyard (Matt 20:1–16), special to Matthew's gospel, those who

arrived in the vineyard late receive the same compensation as those who had "borne the burden of the work and the heat of the day." In the parable of the Two Sons (21:28–32), also found only in Matthew, it is the son who initially rebelled who is eventually commended for his obedience. Although the parable of the Vineyard Tenants (21:33 43) is found in the Synoptic Gospels, only Matthew includes Jesus's concluding application to Israel that "the Kingdom of God will be taken away from you and given to a people who will produce its fruit" (21:43). In the parable of the Wedding Feast (22:1–14) those who were invited to the banquet were too preoccupied to come, so they were instructed to go out into the street corners to bring in those who had not been initially invited. Similar points can be observed in the parable of the Ten Virgins (25:1–13), the parable of the Talents (25:14–30) and the parable of the Sheep and the Goats (25:31–46).

Matthew also includes accounts of Jesus healing non-Jews, including the servant of a Roman Centurion (8:5–13) and the two demon possessed men from the region of the Gadarenes (8:28–34). Clearly, Matthew is interested in pointing out how God's grace extends beyond the particularity of his covenant with Israel.

6. Matthew's Apocalypse. Matthew 24–25 records the fifth and final major discourse in Matthew's Gospel. This last discourse focuses on the end times. After discussing many of the tumultuous signs that will accompany the end such as war, famines, earthquakes, false prophets and the increase of wickedness, Jesus encourages his disciples to "stand firm to the end." Then, in verse 14, Jesus declares, "and this gospel of the kingdom will be preached in the world as a testimony to all nations, and then the end will come." Verse 14 is a statement of optimism and hope about the final outcome as Jesus reveals the full, universalistic mission of his church to "all nations."

Matthew's Great Commission

In light of this brief survey of these themes in Matthew's gospel, it should be clear that the final commissioning of Jesus to his disciples (28:18–20) flows naturally out of the larger context of his gospel. Jesus addresses the disciples, saying, "all authority in heaven and on earth has been given to me" (28:18). This is a widely neglected phrase in discussions concerning Matthew's commission. We are so eager to move on to the actual commission that we fail to see the important theological basis upon which the entire commission is being built. The commission of 28:19–20 is built upon the foundation of a prior understanding of who Jesus *is* and what He has been given prior to this encounter in Galilee. The commission begins and ends with an affirmation of Jesus's presence, and the divine authority that this entails. In other words, Jesus's *being* precedes the church's *doing*, a point too easily forgotten by a task-oriented church. Jesus is shown as the recipient of all authority in heaven and on earth, quite separate from any human response or church-based initiative.

Jesus's words are a clear allusion to Daniel 7 where the Son of man was brought into the presence of the Ancient of Days. The prophet Daniel declares that, "He was given authority, glory and sovereign power; all peoples, nations and people of every language worshipped him" (Dan 7:14). It is this phrase that situates the sending of Jesus within the context of the *missio dei*. It is the Father who has bestowed authority and power and glory upon Jesus. It is the Father who has determined that all nations will ultimately worship Jesus Christ as Lord (Phil 2:9–11), thus placing this commissioning within an eschatological context. In Galilee, the eschatological worship of the nations is already breaking into the present order. The disciples are sent out as heralds of this good news. Thus, Jesus's sending of his disciples in 18:19–20 must be understood within the larger frame of the Father's action and initiative. This has important implications for marketplace ministries that are all under the scope of the authority of Christ and the mission of the church.

In 28:19–20a Jesus says, "go and make disciples of all nations, baptizing them in the name of the Father, and of the Son and of the Holy Spirit, teaching them to obey everything I have commanded you." This part of the commission is organized around the central command to "make disciples" (μαθητεύσατε) which is the only imperative found in the entire passage. In fact, this is the only time in his gospel that Matthew places the verb "to disciple" in the imperative. The command to "make disciples" is surrounded by three supporting participles: going, baptizing and teaching. The participles are descriptive, assuming a church that, in the presence of the Risen Lord, will be characterized by the ongoing actions of going, baptizing and teaching. In the acts of going, baptizing and teaching, Jesus expects his disciples to replicate the eschatological community known as the church among all nations.

The phrase πάντα τὰ ἔθνη "all the nations" (i.e., ethnic groups) has received considerable attention in contemporary missions books. The focus on the precise meaning of this phrase is widely attributed to the writings of Donald McGavran (1897–1990) and Ralph Winter (1924-2009). Donald McGavran's *Bridges of God* published in 1954 followed by his *Understanding Church Growth* in 1970 helped to revolutionize missionary thinking from a focus on *places*, to a focus on planting the church among *people-groups*. In 1974, Ralph Winter gave a paper at the first Congress on World Evangelization held in Lausanne that is regarded as a turning point in contemporary missions. His paper was entitled, "The Highest Priority: Cross-Cultural Evangelism." The paper emphasized the presence of thousands of people-groups who were beyond the current reach of the church and would never be reached without some cross-cultural initiative. This focus on people-groups is based on the recognition that Jesus commands us in Matthew 28 to make disciples of 'all nations.'…[6] The word ἔθνη refers to neither geography nor political entities. The phrase indicates social and ethnic groupings of peoples. It is a phrase captured well by the phrase, "people-groups." This is significant because it recalls the language found in the Abrahamic covenant whereby God promises to extend a blessing to all the "extended families" or "ethnic groups" of the world.

It is also important to note that Jesus does not render the command with the individualistic emphasis of popular interpretation, "make disciples of all the individuals within nations," but the more daunting, holistic command to "make disciples of the nations." In other words, the entire notion of what constitutes our social and ethnic identity as peoples must be brought under the Lordship of Jesus Christ. As Andrew Walls has pointed out, "national distinctives, the things that mark out each nation, the shared consciousness and shared traditions, and shared mental processes and patterns of relationships, are all within the scope of discipleship." Christ must become "visible within the very things which constitute nationality."[7] The implications of this for marketplace ministry are profound. We could actually translate this as "go into every person's world" meaning the world of the lawyers, the world of the school teachers, the world of the artists and film makers, the world of the scientists, and so forth. The Great Commission is more than a call to personal evangelism on a global scale. It is a call for Jesus's disciples to create "communities of obedience among the nations."[8] As the Risen Lord, Jesus concludes the commission by promising his ongoing presence with the community, which is the distinguishing mark of his disciples (Matt 28:20).

Mark: In the Midst of Suffering, Preach the Gospel to All Creation

Although Mark is the second gospel in the New Testament canon, it is widely regarded as coming into being prior to Matthew's gospel. Therefore, Mark's gospel contains several of the themes regarding a universalistic mission which were carried over into Matthew's gospel and have already been explored, such as the Parable of the Vineyard Tenants (Mark 12:1–12), the mini-Apocalypse of Mark 13 which, like Matthew, records that "the gospel must first be preached to all nations (Mark 13:10), Jesus's ministry in Gentile regions (Mark 7:24–30; 8:28–34), and the confession of faith by the Gentile centurion at the crucifixion of Christ (Mark 15:39). Mark also anticipates a worldwide mission when Jesus commends the woman who poured an alabaster jar of expensive perfume on his head. Jesus declared that "wherever the gospel is preached in the whole world, what she has done will also be told, in memory of her" (Mark 14:9).

All four gospels record Jesus cleansing the Temple (Matt 21:12–13; Mark 11:15–17; Luke 19:45–46; John 2:13–16). However, Mark places more of an emphasis on the universal mission to the Gentiles in his record of the cleansing of the Temple. Mark is the only one of the gospel writers who records the final phrase of the citation from Isaiah 56:7, "my house will be called a house of prayer *for all nations*."[9] Jesus is, of course, quoting Isaiah's declaration that the Temple would be "called a house of prayer for all nations" (56:7) which is followed by the affirmation that not only will the Sovereign Lord gather the exiles of Israel, but he will "gather still others to them besides those already gathered" (Isaiah 56:8). The theme of the nations being gathered is a central theme in the original covenant to Abraham.

Mark's Anonymous Great Commission

The oldest manuscripts of Mark's gospel conclude at 16:8, which is, by all accounts, an unnatural and abrupt ending both theologically and linguistically. The absence of a natural conclusion from the earliest manuscripts, coupled with the fact that both of the newer endings (16:9–20 or 16:9–10) contain peculiarities of vocabulary and style which are uncharacteristic of Mark, raises serious doubts about whether the final commission as it appears in our received text is the original.[10] Some scholars are convinced that Mark 16:8 represents the original conclusion to Mark's gospel.[11] It is also possible that Mark's original ending has been lost and that the current ending(s) to Mark's gospel represents an attempt by the early church to restore the original account. It is worth noting that Mark does record Jesus preparing his disciples for a post-resurrection appearance. In Mark 14:28 Jesus says, "after I have risen, I will go ahead of you into Galilee." It seems odd, therefore, that Mark would omit any resurrection appearances at all.

We have, therefore, received an anonymous ending to Mark's Gospel that includes a final commission from our Lord. The very fact that the early church chose to restore the lost ending underscores their understanding concerning the importance of the final commission as the proper culmination of the gospel. Therefore, while understanding this as a later addition, a few observations will be made with a special emphasis on those themes that are present in Mark's gospel.

First, the only imperative found in the passage is the word "proclaim" or "preach" (16:15). The passage commands the church to proclaim the good news to "all creation." This is particularly worth noting since proclamation/preaching is, in fact, a central theme in Mark's gospel. John preaches a baptism of repentance (1:4). Mark does not record any birth narrative, but instead gives us our first glimpse of Jesus in Galilee "proclaiming the good news of God" (1:15). Mark also records Jesus "preaching in their synagogues" and telling his disciples that they must go to nearby villages "so I can preach there also. That is why I have come" (1:38–39). Twice Mark records Jesus sending out his disciples to preach the gospel (3:14; 6:7–12). Proclamation or preaching is clearly a major theme in Mark's gospel.

Second, like Matthew's gospel, the text places the command within an eschatological context warning that whoever believes "will be saved" whereas whoever does not believe "shall be condemned." Mark's entire gospel is set within an eschatological tension which is evident in his emphasis on the end of the world, the destruction of the temple, and the coming persecution of those who preach the gospel (13:1–27).

Finally, the text assumes that miraculous signs will accompany the worldwide preaching of the gospel, including driving out demons, speaking in tongues, laying hands on the sick and being unharmed by snakes or poisons. Mark's gospel, along with all the accounts of Jesus's ministry, emphasizes the miraculous ministry of Jesus. However, Mark is particularly interested in demonstrating that the miraculous ministry of Jesus is replicated in the lives of the disciples, including casting out demons (3:15; 6:13) and healing the sick (6:13).

Looking at the anonymous ending as a whole it is important to recognize that although it may be a restored ending, the central themes are all consistent with Mark's gospel. Mark understood the church as an eschatological community, empowered and equipped supernaturally by the Risen Christ with a universal gospel to proclaim to the whole world.

Luke-Acts: Holistic and Empowered Witnesses of God's Mighty Deeds

Luke's Gospel and Holistic, Empowered Witness

It is important to reflect upon the two commissions that Luke offers in Luke 24:45–49 and Acts 1:7–8 within the larger setting of his writings, as well as within the larger context of the *missio dei*. The ongoing mission of those who follow Jesus is central to Luke's understanding of the church. This is particularly evident since he is the only gospel writer to write a companion volume, the book of Acts, which continues the story, demonstrating how the gospel continues to unfold after the resurrection at Pentecost, and in the ongoing witness of the church.

Luke addresses both his gospel and the book of Acts to a gentile, Roman official named Theophilus (Luke 1:3; Acts 1:1), and it is evident throughout both books that Luke has a predominantly Gentile audience in mind. Thus, Luke re-tells the gospel story in light of the growing Gentile presence in the church. He emphasizes Jesus's interactions with Gentiles, with women, with the poor and others, like tax-collectors and Samaritans, who were marginalized. We will begin by exploring a few selected themes in Luke's gospel in order to set the final commissions in context. The focus here will be on Luke's gospel, with the opening commission of Acts as a bridge from the gospel to the book of Acts.

1. <u>Jesus's Presentation at the Temple</u>. Luke is the only gospel writer who records Jesus's presentation in the Temple. The presentation and sacrifice on behalf of a child was a customary act of

obedience to the Jewish Law as outlined in Leviticus 12. The surprise comes when Simeon, a devout and righteous Jew, is moved by the Holy Spirit to go into the temple courts and bless the child. His prayer of blessing, known as the *Nunc Dimittis* ("Now, dismiss [your servant]…") is a powerful affirmation of the future universalistic mission to the Gentiles. Simeon declares that the Lord can now "dismiss his servant in peace" because his eyes have seen the salvation of the Lord. The infant Jesus is then declared to be "a light for revelation to the Gentiles and for glory to your people Israel" (2:32).

2. <u>John the Baptist's Ministry of Preparation</u>. Not only do all four gospels record the ministry of John the Baptist in preparing the way for the ministry of Jesus Christ, but also they all specifically record his citation from Isaiah 40. However, Matthew, Mark and John are quite succinct in their recording of John's use of Isaiah. John is "a voice of one calling in the desert, prepare the way for the Lord, make straight paths for him" (Matt 3:3; Mark 1:3; John 1:23), quoting from Isaiah 40:3.[12] However, only Luke quotes the entirety of Isaiah 40:3–5. This portion includes not only the familiar theme of valleys being filled in, mountains being made low and crooked places being straightened, but also the declaration that "*all humankind will see God's salvation.*" Through this quotation, Luke confirms the declaration of Simeon about "revelation to the Gentiles," and anticipates the day when "all humankind" would see God's salvation.

3. <u>Holistic Mission</u>. Luke records that Jesus's ministry is inaugurated in Galilee, at the synagogue in Nazareth. Jesus takes the scroll (Luke 4:18–19) and reads Isaiah 61:1–2 from the prophet Isaiah. Then, in dramatic fashion, Jesus declares, "Today this scripture is fulfilled in your hearing" (Luke 4:21). This is how Luke sets the agenda for his understanding of Jesus's mission. With this one quotation, Jesus lays claim to a holistic vision that includes his liberating power in an economic context (the poor), a political context (prisoners and oppressed) and a physical context (the blind).[13] This concern for justice and a holistic perspective on salvation becomes a prominent theme in Luke's gospel and, once again, has enormous implications for marketplace ministries. The "scope" of Jesus's redemptive work is not merely in the privatized interiority of the human heart, but the whole public square of human life and culture. Luke would resist western attempts to overly spiritualize Luke's emphasis on the poor and the downtrodden. Jesus's ministry really does represent good news for the

economic poor. In passages unique to Luke's gospel, we read how He has "filled the hungry with good things, but sent the rich away empty" (Luke 1:53). We hear how the poor man Lazarus rests secure in Abraham's bosom, while the rich man is in agony (Luke 16:19–31). In a passage he shares with the other Synoptic Gospels, Luke records Jesus telling the rich young ruler to "sell everything you have and give to the poor" (18:22).

Luke frequently portrays Jesus in solidarity with the disenfranchised and outcasts of society, including women (13:10–17), tax collectors and sinners (5:29–31; 15:1–32; 19:1–10) and Samaritans (10:30–37; 17:11–19). Many of these texts are unique to Luke's gospel, such as his healing of the crippled woman, the parable of the Good Samaritan, and the parable of the Prodigal Son.

4. <u>Universalistic Mission in Luke</u>. Luke is widely known for his special interest in Gentiles. Not only does Luke record Jesus's ministry outside of ethnic Israel (Luke 8:26–39; 9:51–56), but he puts a personal face on Gentiles who respond favorably to Christ. Some of these pericopes have already been explored in the context of Matthew's gospel. However, there are several accounts reflecting this theme that are unique to Luke's gospel. Luke highlights the faith of "Naaman the Syrian" (4:27), the faith of "the widow in Zarephath in the region of Sidon" (4:26), and the faithfulness of the Samaritan in the Parable of the Good Samaritan (10:25–37). Luke is the only gospel writer who, in the Parable of the Wedding Banquet, records a *second* call to the uninvited. In the first call, they bring in the "poor, crippled, the blind and the lame" (14:21). In the second call, the master sends his servants out again to "the roads and country lanes...so that my house will be full" (14:23). As noted above, Luke alone records the one thankful Samaritan among the ten lepers that were healed who returns to give thanks (17:11–19). Luke, writing to Gentiles, wants to emphasize the favorable response of the Gentiles to the ministry of Jesus. Indeed, Luke is the only gospel writer who prophetically presents the time between Christ's first and second coming as the "times of the Gentiles."[14]

Luke's Great Commission

In light of this brief overview of key themes in Luke's gospel, the final commissioning in Luke 24:46–49 and at the beginning of Acts in

1:7–8 will be considered. Luke's Great Commission which appears in his gospel takes place in Jerusalem on the night after the Resurrection and is, therefore, considerably earlier than Matthew's commission which occurs in Galilee some weeks after the Resurrection.[15] The commission that appears in Acts 1:7–8, in contrast, occurs last among all the other gospels, taking place in Bethany just prior to Christ's Ascension.[16] The unifying feature of both of the commissions recorded by Luke is on the sovereignty of God in missions. The church's initiative and action can only be seen through the lens of the *missio dei*. This emphasis becomes evident in three main ways.

    1. <u>Luke's commissions in the context of God's mission</u>. First, Luke emphasizes the inability of the disciples to understand apart from God's prior action. Luke's gospel commission is preceded by Jesus's resurrection appearance to two of his followers on the road to Emmaus. They are all walking along together, but the text says, surprisingly, "they were kept from recognizing him" (24:16). It is not until Jesus broke the bread that "their eyes were opened and they recognized him" (24:31). Luke emphasizes that their recognition was a result of an act of divine self-disclosure. This finds a remarkable parallel in the appearance to the Apostles later that night. The disciples also did not recognize him, thinking they saw a ghost (24:37). It is later when he "opened their minds so they could understand the Scriptures" (24:45) that they finally began to understand. The same verb for "open" (διανοίγω) is used in 24:31 when the two on the road to Emmaus had their eyes opened and in 24:45 when the disciples' minds were opened. The truth of the gospel is realized only in response to a prior divine self-disclosure. The use of this verb "open" (διανοίγω) to describe the opening of one's eyes, or mind, to understand the Scriptures, or Jesus's identity, is unique to Luke's gospel.[17] The only other occurrence of the word used in this way, is also by Luke in Acts when he records how God "opened" the heart of Lydia to respond to the message of Paul (Acts 16:14). This theme is also evident in Luke's commission in Acts. In Acts 1:7 Jesus says that it is not for us to know "the times and dates the Father has set by his own authority." The emphasis is on the action of God in unfolding his mission, in His time.

    Second, Luke has a strong emphasis on the witness of the church as a fulfillment of (and in continuity with) the Old Testament. Jesus appears to his frightened disciples, shows them his hands and feet, and eats a piece of broiled fish in their presence, dispelling the notion that he was an apparition. Jesus then says, "this is what I told you while I was still with you: Everything must be fulfilled that is written about me in the Law of Moses, the Prophets and the Psalms" (Luke 24:44). This also finds a parallel to the earlier Resurrection appearance on the Road to Emmaus when Jesus walked with two disciples. Jesus admonishes them in a similar fashion, saying, "how foolish you are, and how slow of heart to believe all that the prophets have spoken ... and beginning with Moses and all the Prophets, he explained to them what was said in all the Scriptures concerning himself" (Luke 24:45).

The fulfillment theme continues even within the content of the commissions. Indeed, one of the unique features of both of Luke's commissions is the absence of command forms, which are replaced with the language of fulfillment and God's prior action. In Luke's gospel, the future witness of the church is seen as a fulfillment of promises made in the Old Testament, just as the ministry of Christ was in fulfillment of the Scriptures. In Luke's gospel the commission begins by Jesus's stating, "This is what is written" (24:46). Jesus then seamlessly speaks of his life as well as the church's witness in the context of fulfillment: "This is what is written. The Christ will suffer and rise again from the dead on the third day, and repentance and forgiveness of sins will be preached in his name to all nations, beginning at Jerusalem. You are witnesses of these things" (24:46, 47). The disciples are portrayed as witnesses of God's action in fulfilling the promises of the Old Testament, most notably the Abrahamic covenant, among the nations of the world. The witness of the church is put solidly in the frame of God's mission and his action to fulfill his promises. In the commission in Acts, the witness of the disciples is portrayed as the action of God in and through them. "You will receive [λήμψεσθε] power ... and you will be [ἔσεσθε] my witnesses in Jerusalem, and in all Judea and Samaria, and to the ends of the earth" (Acts 1:8). This is prophetic language, which the church's later action will be fulfilling.

The third way that Luke places his commissions within the context of the larger frame of God's action is in his emphasis on the inability of the disciples to engage in missions, apart from the empowerment of the Holy Spirit. As noted, there is no command form which "sends" the disciples in either of Luke's commissions. Rather, it is the Holy Spirit who is sent. Instead of the expected command to *go*, Jesus tells the disciples to "*stay* in the city until you have been clothed with power from on high" (24:49). That same admonition given on the night after the Resurrection is recalled in the book of Acts, "do not leave Jerusalem, but *wait* for the gift my Father promised, which you have heard me speak about. For John baptized with water, but in a few days you will be baptized with the Holy Spirit (Acts 1:4,5). In Luke/Acts, the Holy Spirit is "the catalyst, the guiding and driving force of missions."[18]

    2. <u>Witnesses of God's Mighty Deeds</u>. The second major theme that emerges out of the commissions in Luke and Acts is the emphasis on the church as witnesses. The word "witness" (μαρτύς) is unique to the commissions in Luke and Acts. In fact, the church as a community of witnesses is one of the unifying themes that link the Gospel of Luke with the Book of Acts (Luke 21:13; 24:48; Acts 1:8, 22; 2:32; 3:15; 5:32; 10:39, 41; 13:31; 22:15; 26:16). A witness is someone who testifies to what they have seen and heard. Jesus said that they would be "witnesses of these things" (24:48) and the record of the book of Acts demonstrates their faithfulness in bearing witness to God's mighty deeds. This is a vital insight for marketplace ministries because Luke does not utilize the normal "church language" of preaching, teaching, and discipling. Rather, he uses a word for the whole people of God, namely, bearing witness. Everyone bears witness, even if you are not gifted for preaching or teaching.

John: The Sending Sent One

John's gospel is written to persuade unbelievers to affirm the Lordship of Jesus Christ, and, therefore, is cast entirely in a missional framework. John writes, "these are written *so that you may believe* that Jesus is the Christ, the Son of God, and that by believing you may have life in his name" (John 20:31).[19] John also has universalistic passages that demonstrate God's light to the nations. John, in his prologue declares that Jesus is "the true light that *gives light to every man* was coming into the world" (1:9). It is John who records that verse which Martin Luther called the "gospel in miniature" and which is regarded as the most well known verse in the New Testament: "For God *so loved the world* that he gave his one and only Son..." (3:16). He is the one who records Jesus revealing himself as the Messiah to a Samaritan woman (4:21–26) and that many Samaritans "believed in him" (4:39). In a profoundly universalistic saying, John records Jesus saying, "I have other sheep that are not of this sheep pen" (10:16). Many more examples could be given. However, the central theme out of which his Great Commission flows is the emphasis on the Sending Father and the Sent Son.

The Sending Father in John's Gospel

John's understanding of mission is primarily found in his use of the verb 'to send' (πέμπω or ἀποστέλλω). John's entire gospel is structured around the Father sending John the Baptist, sending Jesus, sending the Holy Spirit, and culminating in the sending of the church. The verb "to send" in John's gospel contains two ideas, one internal and external. Internally, it "implies a personal relationship," namely, that those who are sent are sent by somebody. Externally, it implies that the one who is sent is "sent for some purpose."[20] John the Baptist is sent as a witness to the arrival of the Messiah: "There came a man who was sent from God; his name was John (1:6). John sees himself as personally sent by God the Father and his purpose is to testify or bear witness to the fact that Jesus is the Son of God. John was not the light, but "he came only as a witness to the light" (1:8). Ten times the gospel describes the purpose of John the Baptist's mission as one sent to bear witness to Christ (1:7 [2x], 8, 15, 19, 32, 34; 3:26, 28; 5:33).

When Jesus steps onto the historical stage in John's gospel, he uses the same language as John, declaring that He was sent by the Father. Like John the Baptist, Jesus uses the "sent" language in both its personal and missional sense. The intimacy between the Son and the Father and the sense of purpose and mission for which he was sent are conveyed regularly in John's gospel.

John's Great Commission

The 40 references to "sending" in John's gospel all culminate in the Great Commission in John's gospel found in John 20:21. It is the last of forty occurrences of the title "sent one" as applied to Jesus in John's gospel.[21] The setting is identical to that of Luke's gospel, behind locked doors in Jerusalem the evening after the Resurrection. As with Luke's gospel, Jesus's first words of comfort to the disciples are, "Peace be with you," followed by their examination of his hands and feet. However, John alone records the following words of commissioning to his disciples: "Peace be with you! As the Father has sent me, I am sending you" (20:21).

Jesus, as the sent one, now sends the church to continue the Father's mission in the world. There are three important features of Jesus's commission in John's gospel that are important to consider. First, the mission of the church is not a new development, but is a continuation of the ministry of Jesus as the ongoing expression of the Father's redemptive act of sending into the world. The Father's redemptive work is not done with the ministry of Jesus, but continues to unfold in Pentecost, the life of the church in the marketplace, and, ultimately, in the New Creation.

Second, the mission of the church is clearly set within a Trinitarian framework in John's gospel. The Father is the Sender. Jesus, as the sent One, sends the church. The Holy Spirit is imparted to the disciples for His presence, guidance and empowerment of the mission. John records that Jesus breathes on them and says, "receive the Holy Spirit" (20:22). Just as the Father breathed His Spirit into humankind at creation (Gen 2:7), so now Jesus breathes the Holy Spirit on his disciples as a sign and seal of the New Creation.

Third, this commission forms the basis for the ongoing sending ministry of the church in missions today. Just as Jesus, who was sent into the world, becomes a sender, so we who have been sent into the world continue to reflect Jesus's ministry as we send out workers into the harvest field.[22] The church is given the ongoing authority to send workers into the field to announce the forgiveness that comes through repentance, as well as the Father's judgment on those who refuse to repent and believe (John 20:23).

Conclusion

This survey of the final commissions given by Jesus Christ and recorded in all four gospels reveals that the Great Commission is actually multi-faceted. Only by listening to the distinctive message of each do they collectively provide the theological basis for the wide range of redemptive works the church engages in which we call missions. Matthew emphasizes the role of discipleship and planting the church across ethnic and cultural boundaries among every people-group in the world. Although we do not have the original words of Mark's commission, the received version is consistent with Mark's emphasis on perseverance in persecution and the central role of proclamation. Luke's commission emphasizes the importance of Spirit empowered, holistic missions as we bear witness to the ongoing, mighty deeds of God. John's commission emphasizes the sending role of the church. Taken collectively, the commissions demonstrate the Father's initiative in missions. The Father imparts all authority to Jesus in Matthew's gospel. In Luke, the church fulfills only what the Father has promised. In John, the Father sends the son who, in turn, sends the church. Thus, all of the commissions are set within the larger context of the *missio dei* and God's original promise to Abraham that he would "bless all nations on earth" (Gen 22:18).

We must work diligently in our day to recover the full meaning of the Great Commission. This means that we must move beyond a "clerical-centric" interpretation of ministry that focuses only on full time Christian professionals. In its place, we need a "laity-focused" interpretation of ministry that equips all of God's people to be disciples in every sphere of life, especially the work place.

What may this look like in practice? The next chapter provides historical perspectives of the church faithfully embodying the Great Commission in the marketplace. Combining a biblical/theological basis with historical examples will provide solid ground for contemporary entrepreneurial church planters to explore missional innovations today.

---

¹ The phrase "The Great Commission" appears as the first chapter title on page 3 and is used in the text on page 4. Interestingly, the phrase is used collectively to refer to all the gospel mandates and does not single out the Matthean version apart from the others. See *History of the Church Missionary Society*, vol. 1, "The Great Commission" (London: CMS, 1899), 3–4. In the 1895 publication of *A New Programme of Missions* by Luther Wishard, the phrase does not appear. He refers to the Matthew 28:18–20 text as the Lord's "gracious command" (Luther Wishard, *A New Programme of Missions* [New York: Fleming Revell, 1895], 94).

² For a survey of the history of the usage of Matthew 28:18–20, see Jack Davis, "'Teaching Them to Observe All that I Have Commanded You': The History of the Interpretation of the 'Great Commission' and Implications for Marketplace Ministries," *Evangelical*

Review of Theology 25 (2001): 65–80.

[3] For these and several other quotations describing the closing pericope of Matthew's gospel see David Bosch, *Transforming Mission: Paradigm Shifts in Theology of Mission* (Maryknoll, NY: Orbis, 1991), 57.

[4] All Scripture citations are from the NIV (1984) unless otherwise noted.

[5] James LaGrand, *The Earliest Christian Mission to 'All Nations' in the Light of Matthew's Gospel* (Atlanta: Scholars Press, 1995), 180.

[6] If Jesus had wanted to emphasize geography or political units rather than peoples, there are a whole range of words which he could have used, including ἀγρός (Mark 5:14; Luke 9:12; 23:26), χώρα (Luke 2:8; 4:37; 15:13), δῆμος (Acts 12:22; 17:5; 19:30, 33), βασιλεία (Matt 4:17; 5:20; Mark 1:15; Luke 9:27; John 18:36) or γῆ (Matt 6:19; 11:24; 24:35; Mark 4:28; 13:31; Luke 21:23; John 17:4). The use of ἔθνη does seem to point away from the traditional geographic and political state identities that have dominated missiological writings and discourse for centuries.

[7] Andrew Walls, *The Missionary Movement in Christian History: Studies in the Transmission of Faith* (Maryknoll, NY: Orbis, 1996), 27.

[8] Christopher J. H. Wright, *The Mission of God: Unlocking the Bible's Grand Narrative* (Downers Grove, IL: IVP Academic, 2006), 391.

[9] The omission of the phrase, "for all nations" by Matthew and Luke is not generally regarded by New Testament scholars as an attempt to downplay the universal mission. Rather, the Temple is regarded as a symbol of Israel that is under God's judgment rather than a natural place where the nations will be gathered. In this view, Christ himself is the new Temple and, by extension, the church. See G. K. Beale, *The Temple and the Church's Mission* (Downers Grove, IL: InterVarsity Press, 2004), 169–200.

[10] Neither ending is present, for example, in Codex Sinaiticus or Vaticanus. The shorter ending to Mark's gospel is found in some Greek, Latin, Syriac and Coptic manuscripts. It is as follows: "But they reported briefly to Peter and those with him all that they had been told. And after this, Jesus himself sent out by means of them, from east to west, the sacred and imperishable proclamation of eternal salvation." However, there are many words and phrases in the shorter ending that never appear in Mark's gospel, such as 'briefly' (συντόμως), 'those around Peter' (τοῖς περὶ τὸν Πέτρον), 'told' (ἐξήγγειλαν), 'after-

ward' (μετὰ ταῦτα), 'east' (ἀνατολῆς), 'as far as the west' (ἄχρι δύσεως), 'sent' (ἐξαπέστειλεν), 'sacred' (ἱερόν), 'imperishable' (ἄφθαρτον), 'proclamation' (κήρυγμα), and 'salvation' (σωτηρίας).

[11] If Mark 16:8 is the original conclusion, then the abrupt ending (the last word in the book would be the word 'for') would represent a dramatic stylistic ending to emphasize a church on the move and under persecution with a deliberate attempt to not bring things to a natural, overly tidy, triumphalistic conclusion. Instead, it would emphasize the extreme vulnerability of the Christian church during the persecution of Nero. Matthew emphasizes Jesus's presence with his disciples; Mark emphasizes Jesus's absence—the bridegroom is absent (Mark 2:20), and, instead, we experience the presence of false prophets (13:5, 6, 21, 22). This would provide a heightened need for vigilance, a willingness to endure persecution, and the necessity of living in the expectation of the return of Christ. Luke's gospel emphasizes the ongoing presence and power of the Holy Spirit. Mark's gospel, in contrast, emphasizes the powerlessness of the church in the face of the powers aligned against it. The power of Christ and the final vindication of believers are anticipated only at the second coming of Christ (13:24–26). Until then, believers must persevere in the face of persecution (13:13).

[12] It should be noted that when the gospels quote Isaiah 40:3 they all make the change from Isaiah's general reference to "God" to a more explicit identification with Jesus as "Lord."

[13] William J. Larkin Jr., "Mission in Luke" pages 152–69 in William J. Larkin Jr. and Joel F. Williams, eds., *Mission in the New Testament: An Evangelical Approach* (Maryknoll, NY: Orbis, 1998), 159.

[14] Larkin, "Mission in Luke," 165.

[15] Although it should be noted that one of the features of Luke's gospel is the collapsing of all the final events into a single expression of an Easter narrative. Luke moves almost seamlessly from Easter to the Ascension, collapsing the forty-day period into a single, dramatic conclusion.

[16] To reconcile the place of the ascension with Luke's record in Acts, John Wenham suggests that the ascension of Christ takes place at the "Mount of Olives" which is "as far as the path to Bethany." It is at the summit of the Mount of Olives that Bethany is in view. See John Wenham, *Easter Enigma: Are the Resurrection Accounts in Conflict?* (Eugene, OR: Wipf and Stock, 2005), 121.

¹⁷ I. Howard Marshall, *The Gospel of Luke*, NIGTC (Grand Rapids: Eerdmans, 1978), 905.

¹⁸ David Bosch, *Transforming Mission: Paradigm Shifts in Theology of Mission* (Maryknoll, NY: Orbis, 1991), 113.

¹⁹ For an exposition of this verse as central to our understanding the purpose of John's gospel, see D. A. Carson, "The Purpose of the Fourth Gospel: John 20:31 Reconsidered," *Journal of Biblical Literature* 106.4 (1987): 639–51. Carson argues persuasively that John's gospel is not primarily addressed to Christians who are in dispute with their synagogue leaders, but to unbelievers, primarily Hellenistic Jews, who do not yet know Jesus Christ. Even John 14–17, the least overtly evangelistic portion of the gospel, should be seen, argues Carson, as a testimony that John was not seeking "superficial professions of faith," but those who grow, abide in Christ, and are discipled.

²⁰ James McPolin, S. J., "Mission in the Fourth Gospel," *Irish Theological Quarterly* 36 (1969): 113–122 at 114.

²¹ All the references are as follows: John 3:34; 4:34; 5:23, 24, 30, 36, 37, 38; 6:29, 38, 44, 57; 7:16, 18, 28, 29, 33; 8:16, 18, 26, 29, 42; 9:4; 10:36; 11:42; 12:44, 45, 49; 13:16, 20; 14:24; 15:21; 16:5; 17:3, 8, 18, 21, 23, 25; and 20:21.

²² The "as ... so" construction is crucial to this understanding. As the Father has sent the Son, so the Son sends the church. As the Son sends the church, so the church sends future disciples into the world.

PART III

PRACTICES WITHIN THE CHURCH

CHAPTER 7

Historical Perspective on Entrepreneurial Church Planting

Samuel Lee

Introduction

Integrating economic activity with church planting and missions is not new. As Chapter 5 indicates, a careful study of the Apostle Paul shows that his missionary strategy combined manual work, discipleship teaching as well as church planting.[1] By implicitly transforming the workplace, Paul created opportunities for the formation of new churches and advanced a broader definition of work as a form of ministry. Additionally, he practiced his faith by demonstrating love in the daily affairs of the workplace and marketplace.[2] In this way, the Apostle Paul provides a helpful basis for entrepreneurial church planting (ECP).

Following in the footsteps of Paul, entrepreneurial witnesses have engaged the marketplace in various forms throughout Christian history.[3] A brief investigation into the diverse Christian traditions illuminates this point by addressing the early examples of the Celtic missionaries (6th century), the Benedictines (7th century), the Nestorians (7th century), Martin Luther (16th century), Matteo Ricci (17th century), the Moravians (18th century), John Wesley (18th century), and Hans Nielsen Hauge (19th century). These particular missional movements and historical figures offer fruitful examples of integrating economic activity with missions, including specifically church planting.

This chapter, therefore, explores how God has used Christian entrepreneurs in the marketplace throughout church history. These historical antecedents illustrate the potential of ECP to break the church out of its limited contexts, planting churches in larger networks of relationships in the marketplace.

Historical Precedence of ECP

In the history of Christianity, theological innovators within different Christian traditions have implemented various expressions of entrepreneurial church activities. This section gives a brief survey of Christian movements and figures that engaged in their faith economically, socially, and evangelistically in the marketplace. Here 'the marketplace' implies cultural centers such as the financial sphere—that is, centers that shape and influence the way society operates.[4] By examining these historical examples, we discover that the ECP approach has a viable track record and remains relevant for contemporary praxis.

The Celtic Missionaries (6th century)

Columba, an early Celtic missionary, was a premodern example of a marketplace witness. He and his monks travelled from Ireland to the Scottish Highlands in order to spread the gospel in the kingdoms of the Northern Picts in the 6th century.[5] When Columba and the Celtic missionaries arrived in the highlands, they first sought close relations with powerful political leaders and authorities; after that, they found favor with the local kings and then established spiritually and economically integrated monasteries. Their daily activities at the monastery included prayer, meditation, Bible study, and physical work, but they also labored as evangelists among the Pict people.[6] In particular, based at this center of spirituality, learning, craftsmanship, and trade, Columba and the Celtic missionaries established a loving relationship with local people. This exposed the Picts to Christianity and often led them to believe in Christ.[7] In this way, the Celtic missionaries, motivated by the Great Commandment, sought to usher in a new era of human flourishing through the monastic vision.

The Benedictines (7th century)

Although the Celtic monks from Ireland brought their version of Christianity to continental Europe beginning in the 6th century, Italian monks were travelling in the opposite direction.[8] Augustine of Canterbury[9] and a group of forty Benedictine monks were sent by Bishop Gregory of Rome to evangelize the English.[10] Their approach to ministry was in line with the 'Rule of St. Benedict,' which united spirituality with economic responsibilities.[11] The Benedictines particularly stressed the importance of work in their missional outreach. The Benedictines' main goal of their entrepreneurial activities was to provide a steady financial stream, facilitating a prudent lifestyle.[12] Like the Celtic missionaries, Augustine also made contact with the local leader, King Ethelbert of Kent, and gained his favor. The King allowed Augustine and the monks to proclaim the gospel freely and to establish churches. In the first year of their ministry, they reported baptizing 10,000 Anglos.[13] Benedictine monasteries later became great centers of learning, trade, and community and established a paradigmatic pattern for ECP during the medieval period.[14]

The Nestorians (7th century)

Christianity spread to central Asia and China through a movement of Nestorian merchant missionaries.[15] Beginning in the 3rd century, Christianity was introduced in Persia, and the Arbela Kingdom and Edessa served as missionary training centers. Although monasticism occasionally was characterized by extreme asceticism, the Nestorian church nevertheless stressed mobility and mission. In the 5th century, Sassanid Persia had opened trade connections with China. Later Nestorian missionaries followed and might have been able to accompany the Persian embassies to China.[16] When they entered into China, Nestorian missionaries identified with the local community by creating economic activities and sharing their faith.[17] In 635, the Nestorian missionary Alopen arrived in the Tang dynasty's capital Changan on the old Silk Road. After Alopen's third year in residence (638), the King decreed toleration. During a period of religious toleration, the first church was dedicated.[18] An important monument dating from 781, unearthed near the ancient capital in 1623, historically substantiates Alopen's arrival. Consequentially, the Nestorian missionaries' evangelistic and missional efforts significantly contributed to promoting the growth of churches in China from the 7th to the 10th centuries.[19] Moreover, these efforts were combined with business acumen.

In sum, these three monastic movements—the Celtic missionaries, the Benedictines, and the Nestorians—offered a balance between work and spirituality in the communities. Yet how did these monasteries, noted for their 'separation' from the world, contribute to the Christian mission? Because monasticism is regarded as a solitary vocation of prayer and asceticism, it is often assumed that the Great Commission was buried under the contemplative goal of becoming righteous before God.[20] Although the hermit school of monasticism emphasizes an isolated spiritual journey, in the history of the church the majority of the monks have been 'coenobitic,' that is, communal. Thus, as we saw above, the Celts, the Benedictines, and the Nestorians built communities of monks as a viable means of spiritual growth for the common good, and they demonstrated neighborly love to unbelievers by combining economic activity, education, and trade. Interestingly, all three monastic communities had a uniquely positive attitude toward wealth. Wealth was understood as a grace bestowed upon the community by God and seen as a useful tool for the purpose of spreading the faith. They also thought of the proper management of wealth as a reflection of holiness. Thus, spiritual asceticism was expressed in their communal economy because members subordinate their own interests to those of the community.[21] As a result, these monastic communities became instrumental in bringing about significant social transformation in Ireland, England, and Asia.[22]

Martin Luther (16th century)

As we move forward chronologically, the Protestant Reformation of the 16th century is understood to have recovered the notion of the priesthood of all believers, thus transforming the understanding of vocation.[23] Since Martin Luther accentuated the universal call of all Christians to service in the world, the theological impetus was on calling and vocation. Luther taught that all Christians, whether carpenters, farmers, or homemakers, were to act as ministers serving their neighbors in consideration of their needs.[24] That is, one's calling is to serve in one's station in life.[25] This theological perspective deconstructed the pervasive sacred/secular distinctions of the Medieval Ages, in which a calling only applied to the priesthood or the monastery.[26]

Instead, Luther's doctrine of vocation relocated religious life into the realm of ordinary life.[27] These insights also recast Luther's own life and ministry; he rejected the monastic lifestyle and married. He also established a printing shop[28] that played a significant role in publishing his writings and spreading the Protestant Reformation. This led to the formation of diverse Reformed churches. Eventually, due to Luther's biblical rediscovery of the priesthood of all believers and his perspective on work as a holy calling, the 16th century was a time of gaining greater confidence in ordinary callings.[29] However, the reduction of calling to one's station in life partly had the negative effect of inhibiting spiritual mobility and reducing perceptions of the need for cross-cultural missionary service.[30]

Matteo Ricci (17th century)

The emergence of Protestantism further illuminated the need for ecclesial reform within the Catholic Church. Of particular importance for this study was the creation of new religious orders to expand Catholic witness in the world. Ignatius Loyola helped form the Society of Jesus (the Jesuits) in 1540 partially out of cross-cultural missional aspirations.[31] The 17th century was an outstanding triumph for Jesuit expansion: Roberto Nobili in India, Matteo Ricci in China, and Alexander de Rhodes in Vietnam.[32] Among these, Matteo Ricci is a good example of a marketplace witness.[33]

Ricci is well known as one of the first contextualists, adopting the look of Confucian scholars seeking to win the Chinese intelligentsia and to make Christianity understandable in the Confucian culture. To do so, he adapted indigenous cultural forms into his Christian witness. For example, he chose the existing Chinese terms for God (T'ien and Shang Ti).[34] He allowed the context to influence the forms of the Christian faith. Additionally, he combined his highly contextualized missionary tactics with his marketplace skills as a "mapmaker, translator, watchmaker, and general scientist."[35] This entrepreneurial approach helped him plant a church that stood the test of time. At his death, there were 400 converts. Within fifty years, another 150,000 were added to the Catholic fold. Ricci made a difference in the Chinese understanding of Christianity that continues to influence Christianity in China today.[36]

The Moravians (18th century)

In the Protestant world after the Reformation, there was little time for thought of cross-cultural missionary activity outside of Europe.[37] A popular view in 16th and 17th centuries among the Protestants was that the command of Christ to preach the gospel to all the world ceased with the apostles.[38] During the 18th century, however, some missional movements arose in terms of integrating business and missions consisting of evangelism and church planting. These movements included Moravianism, the Wesleyan/Evangelical revival, and later, Hans Nielsen Hauge's Society of Friends. These movements served as a "launching pad for Protestant missions."[39] At the close of the 19th century, due to the influence of these movements, the European colonies, North America, and Norway witnessed a phenomenal growth of converts as new Christian communities came into existence.

Perhaps the Moravians were the best-known 18th century example of integrating faith, work, and economics.[40] In the wake of the Reformation, Protestants tended to emphasize the Creation Commission (stewardship and human development), but on the eve of the Evangelical Revival, the Moravians began to spread cross-culturally as they faithfully sought to live out the Great Commandment in obedience to the Great Commission. Influenced by the mission of Hans Egede to Greenland, beginning in 1732 the Moravian churches stepped into missionary work. The Moravian community sent out their missionaries to the island of Saint Thomas in the Caribbean to establish a mission for African slaves.[41] After one of the missionaries used his carpentry skills to support himself, other missionaries soon followed his example. Later all Moravian missionaries were expected to support themselves financially and give any profit they earned from their endeavors to the mission.[42]

The Moravian economic model for missions eventually resulted in the establishment of a large commercial operation in Suriname on the northern coast of South America. The Moravians discovered that business could function as a means of gospel proclamation through a relational connection. For example, while employing African slaves in a tailor shop, the missionaries found it easy to talk about the gospel. Later, in Suriname the establishment of seven churches (with a collective worshipping attendance of 13,000) and a department store fostered holistic transformation.[43] In this way, the Moravians skillfully combined evangelistic efforts with trade and industry, not only providing for their own support, but also helping the local people financially and spiritually.

John Wesley (18th century)

Through the influence of the Moravians,[44] John Wesley also pursued a public society via entrepreneurial means in order to form Christ-following communities. Upon realizing there were large groups of people who were not coming to church, he went to where the masses gathered—the market place, the brickyards, and the coalmines—in order to bring them the gospel. For Wesley, the spread of the gospel included the practice of what Theodore Jennings calls 'evangelical economics,' reflecting Wesley's teleological 'inward and outward holiness.'[45] Thus, Wesley emphasized proper stewardship of money as a means to care for the poor and the marginalized. He exhorted the early Methodists 'to gain all one can, save all one can, and yet give all one can'[46] in order to glorify God through the sharing of goods. His entrepreneurial life and ministry illuminates this. For example, Wesley operated his own successful printing shop to disseminate spiritual writings and pamphlets along with his famous book on medical cared called "Primitive Physick."[47] He also "set up apothecary shops so that they [Methodist communities] could buy the best available treatments of the day at the affordable prices."[48] One estimate proposes that Wesley earned as much as 30,000 pounds (6 million dollars today) from his entrepreneurial business.[49] Almost all of this money was invested in the broader Methodist movement.

The spark generated by Wesley's entrepreneurial approach eventually spread rapidly to the American frontier. Methodist circuit riders, such as Francis Asbury, traveled to locations where pioneers lived and worked, and, consequently transformed people's lives for the better, politically, socially, and spiritually.[50]

Hans Nielsen Hauge (19th century)

A lesser-known example of integrating entrepreneurship in a holistic Christian outreach is Hans Nielsen Hauge (1771-1824). He was instrumental in transforming Norway into a modernized and economically thriving Christian nation in the 18th century and early

19th century.[51] In 1796, at the age of 25, Hauge's journey to faith began when he suddenly felt assured of his salvation. This spiritual encounter provoked him to action as he began sharing his message of assurance with others.[52] Traveling through Norway and Denmark, he preached about the importance of having a personal commitment to the Lord. His preaching resulted in the creation of several spiritual societies relationally connected with Hauge as senior leader. These groups (collectively known as the Society of Friends) took on a guild-like demeanor in that they were organized around occupation. For example, there was both a workers' movement and a farmers' movement in Hauge's network.[53]

In addition to emphasizing spiritual renewal, Hauge *also saw the need to educate and equip common people.* For Hauge, running a business and preaching were inseparable. He had an amazing capacity for work, which, combined with his pioneering spirit, made him an entrepreneur par excellence.[54] During the years 1800 to 1804, he established 150 industries across Norway including "fishing industries, brick yards, spinning wheels, shipping yards, salt and mineral mines, waterfall harnessing, paper mills and printing plants."[55] These innovative industries not only created a source of employment for a modernizing people, but also taught them how to support themselves. In turn, Hauge's religious earnestness and aptitude for business resulted in Norway becoming the foremost model for spiritual, social, and economic transformation.[56] Indeed, Hauge's Society of Friends serves as a viable model for ECP in that entrepreneurship and spiritual renewal were seen as two interrelated pathways for holistic transformation.

Interpretation of the Historical Development

We have thus far investigated the historical foundations for ECP. The historical evidence for the use of economic activity or entrepreneurship in mission work is abundant. As we have seen above, a good number of entrepreneurial witnesses and Christian communities have made notable advances in fulfilling God's mission. There were three emergent outlets for participating in the *missio Dei* by these marketplace practitioners, including the Creation Commission (economically), the Great Commission (evangelistically), and the Great Commandment (socially).[57] Interestingly, these brief sketches of entrepreneurial Christian movements and figures demonstrate three overarching frameworks for missional practice in relation to economic activity and missions:

1. 'Business for Holistic Transformation' with a focus on the Great Commandment,
2. 'Business for Human Development' with a focus on the Creation Commission, and
3. 'Business for Saving Souls' with a focus on the Great Commission.[58]

In other words, though the church received and participated in the same mandates (the Creation Commission, the Great Commission, the Great Commandment) throughout history, communities of faith and Christian innovators addressed these three commissions differently with varying emphases (human development/stewardship, evangelism/discipleship, social transformation). These three overarching frameworks for missional practice is reflected in Chart 1 below:

Chart 1—Three Overarching Frameworks for Missional Practice

Name	Focus	Example
Business for Saving Souls	Evangelism/Discipleship	The Celtic missions
Business for Human Development	Human development/Stewardship	The Protestant Reformation
Business for Holistic Transformation'	Social transformation	The Moravians missionaries

For example, the Celtic missions in the 5th century took the form of 'Business for Holistic Transformation' by stressing the Great Commandment (social transformation). Although evangelism and economic activity were present, the core focus of the Celtic missionaries of the 6th century was on neighborly love and social transformation as demonstrated by the Great Commandment. On the other hand, the Protestant Reformation of the 16th century shifted the emphasis to 'Business for Human Development' with a focus on the Creation Commission (stewardship/human development).[59] Instead of restricting grace to those in formal ministry, the Reformers helped the people of God to become faithful stewards of God-given gifts, no matter their vocational calling. Furthermore, during the 18th and 19th centuries, we can see another shift occurring with the focus on 'Business for Saving Souls' with an emphasis on the Great Commission (evangelism/discipleship). As exemplified by the Moravians, Protestant churches began to reconceive the Great Commission as a mandate to be fulfilled. This paradigm shift partially contributed to an expansion in the numerous churches and mission societies, reaching out to people in non-Christian lands for purposes of gospel proclamation, conversion, and church planting.[60]

In sum, Christian missions have historically emphasized one of three foci or frameworks: 'Business for Holistic Transformation' with a focus on the Great Commandment (social transformation), 'Business for Human Development' with a focus on the Creation Commission (stewardship), or 'Business for Saving Souls' with a focus on the Great Commission (evangelism/discipleship).[61]

Recent Applications of ECP

These three overarching frameworks for missional practice have reemerged in the 20th century. Furthermore, in the 21st century several missiologists and church movements have sought to converge the three historic frameworks into one holistic model.[62] Major events such as decolonization, the rise of nationalism, and the cataclysmic destruction of two world wars provided springboards for those changes. After 1945, with the movement toward decolonization in the majority of the world, newly independent nations, such as India and Vietnam, established several laws limiting Christian expansion and church planting. However, restrictions and world events did not end the call of the Great Commission, the Creation Commission, and the Great Commandment. Churches were now faced with the prospect of creating innovative methods for entering and serving in restricted countries. Various mission strategies have been used to capitalize on the growing variety of opportunities available for mission endeavors. Around the middle of the 20th century, scholars such as Doug Sherman, William Hendricks (1990),[63] and R. Paul Stevens (1999)[64] became particularly interested in the role of business as a mission strategy. As a result, Tentmaking, based on Paul's model in Acts 18:1–3, has been reconsidered. Innovative missionaries began to use their specializations to gain access to countries that restricted the church's activities and forbade missionaries from speading the gospel within the context of the Great Commission and the Creation Commission. While this model produced some spiritual and economic fruit, limitations quickly began to surface, especially as a result of the bifurcation between the two bottom lines. Tentmakers often experienced an ethical dilemma as they entered countries officially for work but then unofficially (and often illegally) engaged in evangelistic outreach.[65]

In the latter half of the 20th century, more thought was given to the strategic use of business for God's mission. Several mission agencies realized that restricted-access nations were eager to initiate ecoomic reform and enlarge their business sectors. While these nations would not permit missionaries to enter the country, many welcomed businesspeople. The merit of using business in global missions was taken seriously by a variety of churches and mission organizations. For example, Business 4 Transformation (B4T) was launched by Operation Mobilization leaders for community revitalization and human development by means of creative business endavors. Also, the phrase Business as Mission (BAM) was formally accepted at the Lausanne 2004 Forum Business as Mission Issue Group. This concept of BAM quickly gained momentum in missions circles.[66] BAM has sought to incorporate business to accomplish the Creation mandate and the Great Commission.[67] However, in a similar predicament faced by Luther in the 16th century, an over-enthusiastic stress on the Creation mandate led BAM practitioners to relegate the church to merely one of several sacred venues advancing the Kingdom of God. Furthermore, there was no two-way traffic between missionaries and those who received the gospel and aid. The tendency was for BAM practitioners to see themselves as superior to those they served—often referring to them as 'heathens'—because missionaries were the distributors of both resources and the gospel. The poor heathens became merely objects to receive help or to 'be fixed,' rather than a person looked upon with dignity and empathy.[68]

In recent years, in post-Christendom countries such as the U.K. and US, another term of incorporating business and church planting with a focus on holistic transformation was introduced: Entrepreneurial Church Planting (ECP). This model involves church planting integrated with business in such a way that a synergetic revelation of the Kingdom of God occurs. This new movement is a subset of Fresh Expressions of Church (FXC). This is because, even though ECP adopts a fresh expressions approach, its context is often reduced to the marketplace and it always has to do with entrepreneurial approaches. FXC will be discussed later in more detail in Chapter 9. Chart 2 shows the relationships between Tentmaking, BAM, and ECP.

Chart 2—A Taxonomy of the Relationship between Tentmaking, BAM, and ECP

Models	Differences	Similarities
Tentmaking	Not always church planting, Not only business, but also other fields such as education or medicine Priority: evangelism and discipleship Missionary Enterprise/ all nation	Laity, Faith & Work, Kingdom focus
BAM	Not always church planting, Business focused Priority: business & holistic transformation Unreached people	Entrepreneurship, Laity, Faith & Work, Kingdom focus
ECP	Connected to church planting, Often connected to a church Priority: Engage the marketplace as an unreached & unchurched/ public marketplace venue	Entrepreneurship, Laity, Faith & Work, Kingdom focus

When it comes to the relationship between ECP, BAM, and Tentmaking, ECP is similar in terms of both the integration of business and ministry and its openness to laity having a full role in the ministry. While ECP shares a common concern with BAM and Tentmaking endeavors, its focus differs. Rather than a bifurcated focus on profit or spiritual growth, ECP seeks to unite these two aims by emphasizing loving relationships—with God and with others. Relationships become the central concept because business and church planting occur within the context of the larger networks of public interpersonal connections.[69] Holistic transformation happens as churches are planted and businesses are established in order to create an environment where people can connect with God and others.

In sum, all three economic-ecclesial models (Tentmaking, BAM, and ECP) commonly use business strategies or entrepreneurship to realize the Creation Commission, the Great Commission, or the Great Commandment. In creative-access countries or in a Post-Christendom context, these strategies have become a unique way of fulfilling the mission of God.

Conclusion

This chapter has explored the creative historical approaches for Christian engagement of faith in the marketplace. This historical sampling reveals that a characteristic method of engaging the unchurched and unreached peoples has been through marketplace witnesses. In other words, in the overall history of the Christian movement, God has used innovative individuals, instrumental movements, and seminal ideas in each era for the creative expansion of His Kingdom by combining economic activity with church planting and missions. These historical perspectives are now reemerging at the cutting edge of God's global mission.

Thus, the vision of those who use an ECP model need to align with the *missio Dei* as it offers the possibility for interaction between church planting/missions and economic activity. More specifically, ECP practitioners are to engage in the *missio Dei* as two-way intercultural interactions between whole-life discipleship (the Great Commission: evangelism/discipleship and the Great Commandment: social transformation) and a call to cultivate the world (the Creation Commission: stewardship/human development). In the process of presenting the entire gospel in the larger networks of relationships in the marketplace, ECP proposes an integration of faith, work, and economics. This integration (faith, work, and economics) will enhance the quality of ministry in global churches to reflect a holistic picture of God's working in the world; in this way, Christian communities will be better equipped to experience the entire gospel in their neighborhoods, the larger society, and the world.

---

[1] In much of this, Paul was following the Jewish Rabbinic traditions of labor and trade along with teaching. See Michael Pocock, Gailyn Van Rheenen, and Douglas McConnell, *The Changing Face of World Missions: Engaging Contemporary Issues and Trends* (Grand Rapids: Baker Academic, 2005), 230–32.

² William J. Danker, *Profit for the Lord: Economic Activities in Moravian Missions and the Basel Mission Trading Company* (Grand Rapids: Eerdmans, 1971), 55.

³ See, for example, William J. Danker, *Profit for the Lord: Economic Activities in Moravian Missions and the Basel Mission Trading Company* (Grand Rapids: Eerdmans, 1971); Michael Pocock, Gailyn Van Rheenen, and Douglas McConnell, *The Changing Face of World Missions: Engaging Contemporary Issues and Trends* (Grand Rapids: Baker Academic, 2005); Tom A. Steffen and Mike Barnett, eds., *Business as Mission: from Impoverished to Empowered*, (Pasadena, CA: William Carey Library, 2006); Lowery, James L. 1976. *Case Histories of Tentmakers* (Wilton, CT: Morehouse-Barlow, 1976).

⁴ Greg Forster, *Joy for the World: How Christianity Lost Its Cultural Influence and Can Begin Rebuilding It* (Wheaton, IL: Crossway, 2014), 13.

⁵ Robert L. Gallagher and John Mark Terry, *Encountering the History of Missions: From the Early Church to Today* (Grand Rapids: Baker Academic, 2017), 45–48.

⁶ F. F. Bruce, *The Spreading Flame: The Rise and Progress of Christianity from Its First Beginnings to the Conversion of the English* (Grand Rapids: Eerdmans, 1973), 386–93.

⁷ George G. Hunter III, *The Celtic Way of Evangelism: How Christianity Can Reach the West—Again*, 10th ed. (Nashville: Abingdon, 2000), 54.

⁸ World History, "History of Monasticism." http://www.historyworld.net/wrldhis/PlainTextHistori es.asp?gtrack=pthc&ParagraphID=eje#eje (accessed November 27, 2017).

⁹ This is not Augustine of Hippo, whom people are used to thinking about with the name "Augustine" but who lived in an earlier era.

¹⁰ Stephen B. Bevans and Roger P. Schroeder, *Constants in Context: A Theology of Mission for Today* (Maryknoll, NY: Orbis, 2004), 123.

¹¹ Ksenia Keplinger et al., "Entrepreneurial Activities of Benedictine Monasteries—A Special Form of Family Business?," *International Journal of Entrepreneurial Venturing* 8.4 (January 1, 2016): 1.

¹² R. W. Hiebl Martin and Feldbauer-Durstmüller Birgit, "What Can the Corporate World Learn from the Cellarer?: Examining the Role of a Benedictine Abbey's CFO," *Society and Business Review* 1 (2014): 51–73.

[13] Stephen Neill and Owen Chadwick, *A History of Christian Missions*, Penguin History of the Church 6, 2nd ed. (London: Penguin, 1990), 58–59.

[14] Edward L. Smither, *Mission in the Early Church: Themes and Reflections* (Cambridge: Cascade, 2014), 39–43.

[15] Samuel Hugh Moffett, *A History of Christianity in Asia*, 2nd ed. (Maryknoll, NY: Orbis, 1998), 291, 297, 461.

[16] Moffett, *A History of Christianity in Asia*, 290.

[17] Cynthia Jan Villagomez, "The Fields, Flocks, and Finances of Monks: Economic Life at Nestorian Monasteries, 500–850" (Ph.D., University of California, Los Angeles, 1998), 104.

[18] Moffett, *A History of Christianity in Asia / Samuel Hugh Moffett*, 288; Tom A. Steffen and Mike Barnett, eds., *Business as Mission: from Impoverished to Empowered* (Pasadena, CA: William Carey Library, 2006), 133–46.

[19] Mar Aprem, *Nestorian Missions*: No. 2 (Trichur, Kerala: Mar Narsai, 1976), 18; Dale T. Irvin and Scott W. Sunquist, *History of the World Christian Movement: Earliest Christianity to 1453* (Maryknoll, NY: Orbis, 2001), 278.

[20] Don Fanning, "Brief History of Methods and Trends of Missions," http://digitalcommons.liberty.edu/cgi/viewcontent.cgi?article=1000&context=cgm_missions (accessed November 27, 2017).

[21] Villagomez, *The Fields, Flocks, and Finances of Monks*, 104.

[22] Ralph D. Winter and Steven C. Hawthorne, eds., *Perspectives on the World Christian Movement: A Reader*, (Pasadena, CA: William Carey Library, 2009), 280.

[23] Vinoth Ramachandra, *The Recovery of Mission: Beyond the Pluralist Paradigm* (Grand Rapids: Eerdmans, 1997), 117.

[24] Gene Edward Veith, *Working for Our Neighbor: a Lutheran Primer on Vocation, Economics, and Ordinary Life* (Grand Rapids: Christian's Library, 2016), 13–14.

[25] Ben Witherington, *Work: A Kingdom Perspective on Labor* (Grand Rapids: Eerdmans, 2011), 32.

[26] Roland H. Bainton, *Here I Stand: A Life of Martin Luther* (Peabody, MA: Abingdon, 1990), 156.

[27] Roland H. Bainton, *The Reformation of the Sixteenth Century* (Boston: Beacon, 1952), 246.

[28] Walter G Tillmanns, "The Lotthers: Forgotten Printers of the Reformation," *Concordia Theological Monthly* 22.4 (April 1951): 260-64 at 261.

[29] Mark C. Taylor, *After God (Religion and Postmodernism)* (Chicago: University of Chicago Press, 2009), 65–66.

[30] R. Paul Stevens, *The Other Six Days: Vocation, Work, and Ministry in Biblical Perspective* (Grand Rapids: Eerdmans, 1999), 74–75.

[31] Dale T. Irvin and Scott W. Sunquist, *History of the World Christian Movement*, vol. 2, *Modern Christianity from 1454-1800* (New York: Orbis, 2012), 112–23.

[32] Thomas Banchoff and José Casanova, eds., *The Jesuits and Globalization: Historical Legacies and Contemporary Challenges* (Washington: Georgetown University Press, 2016), 175.

[33] Pocock, Rheenen, and McConnell, *The Changing Face of World Missions*, 233.

[34] Sangkeun Kim, *Strange Names of God: The Missionary Translation of the Divine Name and the Chinese Responses to Matteo Ricci's* (New York: Peter Lang, 2005), 29.

[35] Pocock, Rheenen, and McConnell, *The Changing Face of World Missions*, 233.

[36] Kenneth Scott Latourette, *A History of the Expansion of Christianity* Vol 3, *Three Centuries of Advance*, (New York: Harper & Brothers, 1939), 339–42.

[37] The reasons were 1) the disputes among the Protestants, 2) consolidation of doctrines and stabilization of the church, and 3) *Cuius region, eius religio*, which means that in each area the ruler is responsible for the spiritual welfare for his people. Cf. Ralph D. Winter et al., *Foundations of the World Christian Movement: A Larger Perspective Course Reader* (Pasadena, CA: Institute of International Studies, 2008), 370; James A. Scherer, *Gospel, Church & Kingdom: Comparative Studies in World Mission Theology* (Eugene, OR: Wipf & Stock, 2004), 67.

[38] David Jacobus Bosch, *Transforming Mission: Paradigm Shifts in Theology of Mission* (Maryknoll, NY: Orbis, 1991), 249.

[39] Winter et al., *Foundations of the World Christian Movement*, 370

[40] Pocock, Rheenen, and McConnell, *The Changing Face of World Missions*, 233.

[41] Business as Mission Think Tank Group, *Business as Mission and Church Planting Fruitful Practices for Establishing Faith Communities* (BAM

Think   Tank,   2013),   1–32, http://bamglobal.org/wp-
content/uploads/2015/12/BMTT-IG-BAM-and-CP-Final-Report-
January-2014.pdf (accessed November 27, 2017).

[42] Danker, *Profit for the Lord*, 34.

[43] Herbert Spaugh, "A Short Introduction to the History, Customs,   and   Practices   of   the   Moravian   Church,"
http://newphilly.org/pdf/moravian.ashorthistory.pdf (accessed November 02, 2017).

[44] Wesley admired the Moravians and affirmed this of them,
"you are not slothful in Business, but labour to eat your own Bread,
and wisely manage the Mammon of Unrighteousness, that ye may
have to give to others also, to feed the Hungry, and cover the Naked
with a Garment" (*The Works of the Reverend John Wesley, A.M: Volume V*
[Oxford: J. Emory And B. Waugh, 1833], 166).

[45] See Theodore W. Jennings, *Good News to the Poor: John Wesley's
Evangelical Economics* (Nashville: Abingdon, 1990), 111–16.

[46] John Wesley and Joseph Benson, *The Works of the Rev. John
Wesley, Volume 10* (New York: J. & J. Harper, 1827), 150.

[47] David Wright, *How God Makes the World a Better Place: A Wesleyan Primer on Faith, Work, and Economic Transformation,* (Grand Rapids:
Christian's Library Press, 2012), 71.

[48] Wright, *How God Makes the World a Better Place*, 71.

[49] Charles Edward White, "Four Lessons on Money from One
of the World's Richest Preachers," *Christian History* 7/3.19 (January 1,
1988): 21–24 at 24.

[50] One good example is that Wesley and 19th century
Wesleyanism argued against the vile practice of slavery. In his sermon,
"Thoughts Upon Slavery," he put slavery in a historical context, but
then quickly spoke against the common myth that people are saved
through slavery by bringing them out of a terrible place. He did this by
describing Africa before the slavers came. He spoke about how the
Africans were procured, making sure to describe how appalling it was
and unlike Christian salvation. In order to abolish slavery, Wesley not
only published letters against the evil of slavery but also assisted the
abolitionists in their cause to have parliament outlaw slavery. Wesley's
argument had a considerable impact on the evangelical movements of
19th century America. According to Donald W. Dayton, Charles
Finney continued the movements begun in England by Whitefield and

Wesley (*Discovering an Evangelical Heritage,* 1st ed. [Peabody, MA: Hendrickson, 1988], 88). Wesley was a great evangelist who called for the reformation of humankind. He not only fought against slavery, but he also brought a great deal of impetus to the female role in social and Christian ministry through his revivalism (ibid., 92–93).

⁵¹ A. M. Arntzen, *The Apostle of Norway: Hans Nielsen Hauge* (Eugene, OR: Wipf & Stock, 1933), preface.

⁵² M. O. Wee, *Haugeanism: A Brief Sketch of the Movement and Some of Its Chief Exponents* (St. Paul, MN: The Author, 1919), 22–24.

⁵³ Karina Hestad Skeie, *Building Gods Kingdom: Norwegian Missionaries in Highland Madagascar 1866– 1903,* Studies in Christian Mission (Leiden: Brill, 2012), 20.

⁵⁴ Joris van Eijnatten and Paula Yates, *The Churches, The Dynamics of Religious Reform in Church, State and Society in Northern Europe, 1780– 1920: 2* (Leuven: Leuven University Press, 2010), 264.

⁵⁵ Trevor Saxby, "Revival-Bringer: Hans Nielsen Hauge's Reformation of Norway," https://makinghistorynow.wordpress.com /2017/04/11/the-country-boy-who-fathered-a-nation-part-1/ (accessed November 2, 2017).

⁵⁶ David S. Lim, "Norway: The Best Model of a Transformed Nation Today," Davidlim53's Blog, https://davidlim53.wordpress.com /2011/09/02/norway-the-best-model-of-a-transformed-nation-today/ (accessed November 27, 2017).

⁵⁷ Neill and Chadwick, *A History of Christian Missions,* 22–23; Irvin and Sunquist, *History of the World Christian Movement,* 305–7.

⁵⁸ In their book *Constants in Context: A Theology of Mission for Today,* Bevans and Schroeder identified six constants of mission: Christology, ecclesiology, eschatology, salvation, anthropology, and culture. They summarized the theology of mission under three models: (1) mission as saving souls and extending the church, (2) mission as discovery of the truth, and (3) mission as commitment to transformation. For the purpose of this study, Bevans and Schroeder's theoretical structure was used by adopting their three models. However, Bevan and Schroeder's theoretical structure does not necessarily mean a link to the integration of business and church planting.

⁵⁹ Hans-Werner Genischen, "Luther, Martin," pages 415–416 in *Biographical Dictionary of Christian Mission* (Grand Rapids: Eerdmans, 1998), 416.

⁶⁰ Scherer, *Gospel, Church & Kingdom*, 36.

⁶¹ Samuel Lee, "Can We Measure the Success and Effectiveness of Entrepreneurial Church Planting?," *Evangelical Review of Theology* 40.4 (October 2016): 327-345 "at" 330.

⁶² Jordan J. Ballor, *Ecumenical Babel: Confusing Economic Ideology and the Church's Social Witness* (Grand Rapids: Christian's Library, 2010), xi.

⁶³ Cf. Doug Sherman and William D. Hendricks, *Your Work Matters to God* (Colorado Springs: NavPress, 1990).

⁶⁴ Cf. Stevens, *The Other Six Day*.

⁶⁵ Lee, "Can We Measure the Success and Effectiveness of Entrepreneurial Church Planting?," 330–31.

⁶⁶ Tunehag, McGee and Plummer (Eds), "Business as Mission. Lausanne Occasional Paper #59," 2004, Available at: http://www.lausanne.org/documents/2004forum/ LOP59_IG30.pdf.

⁶⁷ For further discussion, see Lausanne Committee for World Evangelization, "Business as Mission: Lausanne Occasional Paper No. 59" (produced by the Issue Group on this topic at the 2004 Forum for World Evangelization, Pattaya, Thailand, September 29 to October 5, 2004).

⁶⁸ Lalsangkima Pachuau, "Missiology in a Pluralistic World: The Place of Mission Study in Theological Education," *International Review of Mission* 89.355 (October 1, 2000): 540–41.

⁶⁹ Lee, "Can We Measure the Success…?," 334.

CHAPTER 8

Characteristics of Entrepreneurial Church Planters[1]

W. Jay Moon

Introduction

This chapter explores the characteristics of entrepreneurial church
(EC) planters.[2] To accurately portray these church planters who are
also entrepreneurs, however, I will have to first dispel some common
myths about entrepreneurs, and then describe how entrepreneurs
differ from others by the way they think and act. Finally, I will propose
a paradigm for EC planters based on case studies of present EC
planters, which will help us discover characteristics of these planters.

Common Myths about Entrepreneurs

Picture a person who is extroverted, aggressive, highly caffeinated,
Type A, lone ranger, intuitive genius, and an extreme risk taker—many
consider this to be a classic entrepreneur. The only problem is that this
stereotype is *not* supported by data; rather, this portrayal of an
entrepreneur is simply a myth. The stereotype breaks down when
looking at real world examples like Steve Wozniak, co-founder of
Apple, who is highly introverted, evidenced by his own statements, "I
am not the right person for social networks. I was never social in my
life. I am not good at socializing in person."[3] Wozniak is not alone in

the entrepreneurship world. In addition, the following highly successful entrepreneurs are also self-proclaimed introverts:[4]

> Warren Buffett - CEO of Berkshire Hathaway
> Larry Page - Co-Founder and CEO of Google
> Mark Zuckerberg - Co-Founder and CEO of Facebook
> Elon Musk - CEO and Product Architect of Tesla Motors

Although researchers have typically attempted to identify common personality traits for entrepreneurs, recent data has led them to other conclusions. Heidi M. Neck, Christopher P. Neck, and Emma L. Murray explain, "[O]ver the last couple of decades, researchers have moved away from the traits perspective in favor of how entrepreneurs think and act, and have discovered that there are patterns in how entrepreneurs think."[5] Researchers now summarize the following truths about entrepreneurs:

1. Entrepreneurs do not have a special set of personality traits.
2. Entrepreneurship can be taught (it's a method that requires practice).
3. Entrepreneurs are not extreme risk-takers.
4. Entrepreneurs collaborate more than they compete.
5. Entrepreneurs act more than they plan.
6. Entrepreneurship is a life skill.[6]

Each of these truths dispels many misconceptions that people may have about EC planters.

Entrepreneurial Thinking and Acting

Instead of looking for EC planters with particular personality traits, then, we should focus our search toward the patterns of thinking and acting to discover entrepreneurial potential. Researchers have "... discovered that there are patterns in how entrepreneurs think. This means that all of us have the ability to act and think entrepreneurially with practice."[7]

Five key skills that entrepreneurs cultivate are play, experimentation, empathy, creativity, and reflection.[8] The cultivation and demonstration of these skills is what equips people to think and act entrepreneurially. Stanford University psychologist Carol Dweck[9] describes two different types of mindsets: a fixed mindset and a growth mindset. Successful entrepreneurs tend to cultivate the growth mindset. The two mindsets are described as follows:

> In a **fixed mindset**, people perceive their talents and abilities as set traits. They believe that brains and talent alone are enough for success and go through life with the goal of looking smart all the time. They take any constructive criticism of their capabilities very personally, and tend to attribute others' success to luck or some sort of unfair advantage. People with a fixed mindset will tell themselves they are no good at something to avoid challenge, failure, or looking dumb.
>
> On the other hand, in a **growth mindset**, people believe that their abilities can be developed though dedication, effort, and hard work. They think brains and talent are not the key to lifelong success, but merely the starting point. People with a growth mindset are eager to enhance their qualities through lifelong learning, training, and practice. Unlike people with fixed mindsets, they see failure as an opportunity to improve their performance, and to learn from their mistakes. Despite setbacks, they tend to persevere rather than giving up.[10]

It is now apparent that EC planters are not characterized by a particular personality type that we can simply identify; rather, they have developed a particular mindset to help them receive information and then act on that information. This will be helpful as we develop a paradigm for EC planters shortly.

Church Planting and Entrepreneurship

To identify entrepreneurial church planters, then, we are looking for those who have capacity for *both* church planting *and* entrepreneurship. To be clear, these terms are *not* synonymous. Ed Stetzer warns bi-vocational planters, "This dual calling is not for the faint of heart. The sacrifice of two jobs requires even more scrutiny to balance."[11] EC planters need to meet the standard requirements of both church planting and entrepreneurship.[12]

On the one hand, there are many similarities between entrepreneurs and church planters since both…

- o   create what is not there yet by starting with what they have at hand;
- o   take steps in faith (entrepreneurs call it "calculated risk");
- o   seek to create value for other people;
- o   find opportunity (needs) and act on them;
- o   need finance with a regular cash flow;
- o   manage and organize human resources; and
- o   are susceptible to burnout

On the other hand, there are some major differences between church planters and entrepreneurs. Church planters …

- o   depend upon the work of Holy Spirit, not simply a business plan. This requires spiritual insight that is not gained through pro forma financial projections alone.
- o   aim to transform the worldview of others, not simply cater to their needs and desires. Success, then, includes attending to spiritual and social metrics and not simply reaching a single financial bottom line.
- o   recognize that the customer is NOT king. The *missio Dei* motivates the church planter to reveal the kingdom of God so that the church becomes a sign, agent, and foretaste of the kingdom of God for the sake of the world.[13] The church, then, exists not simply to provide spiritual services that are attractive to believers; rather, the church is always challenged to be on mission with God to reach the world, which includes having a prophetic voice in culture.

Prototypical EC Planters

While it may seem like a tall task to find a church planter who is also an entrepreneur, there are several examples to guide us. We have already looked at some historical precedents and biblical examples in previous chapters. In addition, there are significant contemporary examples worldwide in the UK[14], South Korea[15], Africa[16], Asia[17] and the U.S.A.[18] Although there are many examples to study, the following case studies serve to illustrate a common paradigm for EC planters that I have observed in person.

Entrepreneur and educator, Michael Goldsby, developed a paradigm to describe the characteristics of entrepreneurs.[19] After studying many entrepreneurs, Goldsby noted that entrepreneurs were different from others in the way that they both received new information and then acted on that information, resulting in four different types of entrepreneurs. Based on the case studies that I visited, I modified Goldsby's model to describe EC planters in Figure 1 below. The y-axis portrays how these EC planters receive information from Concrete (quantitative data, surveys, statistics, demographics, etc.) to Abstract (qualitative data, preferences, feelings, attitudes, aspirations, etc.). The x-axis describes how these EC planters then act on this information from Connecting (people, places, and disparate ideas together) to Exploring (opportunities, possibilities, and new ideas).

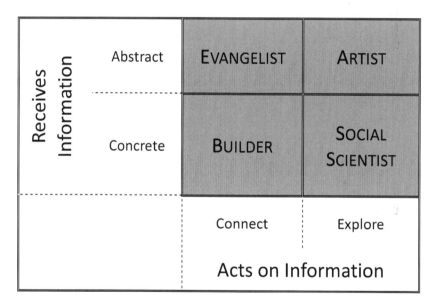

Figure 1—Types of Entrepreneurial Church Planters

A. Artist (Abstract Explorer): The Artist type of EC planter gathers abstract information such as preferences, values, ideals, aspirations, and dreams. Once they receive this information, they act on this by exploring new ideas and possibilities. Chris Sorenson is an example of an Artist entrepreneurial church planter that planted the Camp House in Chattanooga, TN.[20]

The Camp House is a coffee shop and café that serves high quality coffee and food throughout the day. The week that I visited, the Camp House advertised daily evening entertainment with a cover charge. Sitting at one of the tables scattered throughout the building on a Saturday evening, I enjoyed local musicians along with 50-75 others, largely millennials. The lighting near the coffee bar reflected a more contemporary appeal while the lighting and artwork became more "ancient" as one moved closer to the stage that displayed a Byzantine mosaic in the background. This artistic expression of the "ancient-future" church motivated Chris and the church planting team.

On Sunday morning, the tables were moved to the side and rows of chairs were arranged to accommodate roughly 150 people for the Anglican worship service. This ECP has now replicated itself in two other coffee shops in Chattanooga with further expansion plans already in the works.[21]

   B.   Social Scientist (Concrete Explorer): The Social Scientist type of EC planter gathers concrete information such as facts, figures, and demographics but then utilizes that information to explore possible opportunities and ideas. Bob Armstrong is an example of a social scientist that started the Blue Jean Selma church and the Arsenal Place Business Accelerator in Selma, AL.[22]

Judge Armstrong observed the significant problems related to poverty, unemployment, and racism. As a result, he started a church and business incubator as a kingdom strategy to overcome these pressing issues in the city. Six businesses have been incubated so far. The first business, G Mommas Cookies, has now expanded due to its widespread success in sales at all of the Cracker Barrel restaurants nationwide and in Walmart stores across the southeastern United States.

Blue Jean Selma church gathers a very diverse group of 200 people each week. Armstrong notes, "We are black, white, rich, poor, middle class, addicts, bank presidents, the mentally handicapped, doctors, lawyers, blue collar workers, unemployed, young, & old. We are fully integrated."[23] Using the information about the tensions in the city, the Blue Jean Selma church is exploring unique approaches to transform the city as they incubate various businesses in the city.[24]

C. Evangelist (Abstract Connecter): The Evangelist[25] gathers abstract information such as preferences, values, ideals, aspirations, and dreams like the Artist; however, unlike the Artist, the Evangelist uses this information to connect people and places together. Shawn Mikschl is an example of the Evangelist church planter in Nicholasville, KY.

Mikschl intentionally works alongside fellow servers, waiters, and waitresses at a local restaurant in order to understand them through authentic relationships that form through working together. What is unique is that his church meets at 11 PM on Thursday evening since this is the time that they get off work and are available to gather. What is even more intriguing is that this simple church meets at a local bar since previous venues did not prove to be appealing in the past (including Mikschl's own home). While this group has varied in attendance, about 15 people regularly gather for prayer, worship, and Scripture teaching.

D. Builder (Concrete Connecter): The Builder gathers concrete information such as facts, figures, and demographics (like the social scientist). The Builder differs from the Social Scientist, however, in that the Builder uses this information to connect people and places together. Lonnie Riley exemplifies the Builder church planter in Lynch, KY.

Riley observed the deep poverty and despair when he first moved to this former coal-mining town. He initially started to serve the needs of the community through simple acts of kindness, such as hedge trimming, and cookie giveaways. Gradually, he obtained and revitalized several vacated buildings in order to start 15 different businesses and ministries to include a: coffee shop, gas station, hotel, retreat center, fitness center, veterinary clinic, bike rental, community center, educational facility, horse stable, and trolley ride service. This led to a church plant, the Community Christian Center, and revitalization of other churches in the community, as described by Riley, "What started off as a meeting of the Meridzo Center Ministries staff has evolved into a safe and friendly public place for people from all walks of life to gather together for praise and worship, Bible study, and warm family fellowship − all in the name and the loving Spirit of

Jesus Christ."[26] This ministry has resulted in significant transformation of the Lynch community as recently portrayed in the documentary "It's Only Cookie Dough."[27]

Common Tendencies of Prototypical EC Planters

When trying to identify the characteristics of EC planters, there is no single set of personality traits that is common to all. Each of the EC planters mentioned in the four prototypical examples above has very different sets of personality traits. This dispels many of the myths that people often have concerning the ideal entrepreneur. On the other hand, there were several common tendencies under two broad categories that I observed that were common to them all:[28]

1. Initial Motivation:

a. Identify the Need. They all recognized an area that was lacking or needed improvement and wanted to make a change. For most, they were dissatisfied with the status quo, while others had a desire to reverse circumstances forced upon them due to shifts in the community.

b. Wait for God's Direction. They were willing to move slowly as they waited for God to show further direction, and all went through a time of waiting and prayer. This was a period of uncertainty where they really did not know exactly what to do next. They felt a strong call by God (motivating them to step out), but the exact steps were not spelled out so they had to depend on God for daily guidance.

c. Embrace Different Experiences. All had lived in other cultural settings and were willing to move to a new location and take risks. Financial need was sometimes the original motivation, specifically some of the pastors were seeking to support their ministry locally without depending on outside funds. The various cultural experiences fostered new and fresh approaches to nagging problems.

d. Start Where You Are with What You Have. All of the businesses started off small with very simple steps like making cookies, cutting hedges, or repurposing an old building, for example. They used their existing interests, talents, and experiences to build the business (like horseback riding, house construction, or business experience). They found that being faithful in small things led to greater opportunities later.

2. Personal Background

a. Faith Is the Foundation. All had a strong and growing Christian faith. They took calculated risks (not impulsive gamblers though), were not deterred easily (willing to wait for God's direction), were a bit stubborn (not deterred by initial failure or later opposition from the church or community), and most had previous experience in ministry before launching their business.

b. Those Closest to Us Become Our Strongest Assets. They all had connections with outside partners who later came alongside them to assist. One surprise that I found was that many of the EC planters had a spouse with significant business experience. Several described how they relied upon their spouse for daily business such as operations, finance, or accounting. Funding sources also usually came from a close network of friends, family members, coworkers, church members, and larger church connections. Howard Dayton, founder of Crown Ministries and Compass ministry, is adamant that those who are contemplating a business start-up should seek a mentor. He warned, "It's imperative that you pray for the Lord to send you a mentor. This can mean the difference between success and failure."[29]

3. Execution

a. Team Player. All of the above EC planters relied upon a team in order to accomplish the job. Frankly, no individual has the capacity in all of the areas of finance, accounting, organizational planning, management, as well as church planting. As a result, they either recruited a team or had to later seek people with particular skills. For example, Chris Sorenson mentioned, "If I had to do this over again, the first person that I would hire is an accountant." A capable and devoted team with various skills is essential. On a personal note, I have found that a team of EC planters is necessary to avoid burnout.[30]

b. Ready to Pivot. While the EC planters all had some initial ideas about how to go about their ministry, they were open to change based upon what they found. Trial and error with various experiments eventually led to success. Eric Ries describes this as continuous innovation with small-scale experiments in a quick feedback look in his book "The Lean Startup"[31]

Cautions for EC Planters

At this point, it is helpful to point out several cautions that need to be considered by EC planters. These arise from critiques leveled against the social entrepreneurship and Business as Missions (BAM) movements. Three main critiques warn against the marketization of society, functional platforms for shoddy business, and justifying evil via Corporate Social Responsibility (CSR). I will briefly discuss each of these cautions.

First, EC planters must beware of the pervasive *marketization of society*. Marketization is defined by M. Simpson and G. Cheney as "a framework of market oriented principles, values, practices, and vocabularies; as a process of penetration of essentially market-type relationships into arenas not previously deemed part of the market; or as a universal discourse that permeates everyday discourse but largely goes unquestioned."[32] In short, regarding society as simply an open market can dehumanize people as simply customers or objects of exchange and be harmful to relationships. EC planters need to remember that people are more than simply customers. As a result, decisions cannot be simply based on the bottom line of financial profit. Pope Benedict calls for a reimagining of the economic system in favor of a "civil economy" such that "principles other than profit and economic exchange can find a place within the economic activity itself";[33] others call for "compassionate capitalism."[34] EC planters are urged to adopt a triple bottom line: social capital, spiritual capital, and financial capital. In practice, this means that all three of these metrics must be considered for decision-making. It is not sufficient to make a decision, for example, based on financial profit alone; rather, questions must be asked about the effect on social and spiritual capital. This mitigates against the excesses of the free market system and re-humanizes people in a community of compassionate care and mutual exchange.

Second, EC planters must watch out for *functional platforms*. When businesses are simply regarded as functional platforms in order to get access to people, then this may lead to shoddy business practices. The BAM movement in restricted access countries has been accused of this practice at times. Instead of regarding the business as simply a functional device to evangelize people, EC planters need to be reminded that the first act of worship in the marketplace is to do our jobs with excellence. Shoddy business practice is not a credible witness of God's calling upon our lives. Dorothy Sayers says it eloquently, "No crooked legs or ill-fitted drawers ever, I dare swear, came out of the carpenter's shop at Nazareth."[35] Both the inherent worth of the value creation developed by work and the value of evangelism are important and need to both be emphasized in ECP.[36]

Third, EC planters should be discerning of *Corporate Social Responsibility* (CSR). Corporate Social Responsibility has become a popular trend in many businesses for various reasons. This is meant to satisfy customers that the business is actually providing a positive social benefit. While this sounds good, CSR can be used by a non-ethical business practice to justify this practice since they rationalize that they are doing much good in the end. For example, I observed a "Pay Day Loan" that was making loans with exorbitant interest rates, which often led to heavy debt among an at-risk community. They later opened a youth center in the same community in order to demonstrate their CSR! In Christian circles, this can take the form of trying to redeem a harmful business practice by the owners simply using the profit for additional offerings and tithes. John Wesley encountered this problem in the eighteenth-century and developed guidelines for business practices. He noted that the workers should not be physically or mentally harmed, and there should be no harm to society.[37]

Fourth, EC planters take *Wesley's advice*. In addition to the "do no harm" advice of Wesley, he had two other measures to help businessmen and women. First, he encouraged accountability in regular meetings where they were asked to report how much money they made and what they did with it. This accountability encouraged Christians to continually focus on how they were using their profit as a means to create social good instead of simply satisfy the desires of the flesh. Wesley's third principle to help business people was to encourage them to be generous. Of the three commands in the famous statement "gain all you can, save all you can, and give all you can," the latter portion was the hardest to put into practice. He encouraged practicing generosity, though, as a spiritual practice to prevent money from finding a "resting place in your soul." Wesley practiced his own advice and encouraged others to do so, which resulted in successful entrepreneurial church plants amidst the prevailing market economy. Taken altogether, each of the cautions portrayed above remind EC planters that they need adequate balance and reflection with their business. For example, the EC planter should create a robust business model with an effective value proposition based on market segments, considering the supply chain and distribution networks.[38] But, the business must not only be evaluated on profit metrics. The business needs to also consider the triple bottom line. In addition, the business should provide a venue to effectively evangelize and utilize the social networks generated by the business. But, the business must not simply be a platform for shoddy work; instead, it also provides an opportunity to glorify God by excellent products and services that reveal the kingdom of God. Again, the business should be an environment to live out CSR and generously support Christian and charitable causes amidst a watching world. But, it should not only emphasize CSR or giving at the expense of ethical practice; rather, the business must be conducted in a way that reflects Christian ethics and values. The point is this: While each of these cautions is necessary to consider, they should not provide an excuse for the church to abdicate her role in the marketplace. Instead, EC planters wisely move into the marketplace using sound missiology as carefully and sensitively as thoughtful missionaries move into any foreign culture.

Conclusions

It should be clear that the search for an exemplary EC planter is not simply satisfied by finding a set of well-defined personality traits. The EC planters all had different personalities but they had clearly identified patterns of how they received information (from abstract to concrete data) and then acted on this information (from connecting to exploring). They all had a good idea that created value for others. In addition, they built a good team of people with various skills, and they were able to experiment with initial ideas and pivot based upon quick feedback. They each had a strong faith background and were willing to wait in prayer for the Holy Spirit to provide direction, followed by significant steps in faith when the time was right. They also had a growth mindset whereby they recognized needs and started small with what they had through hard work and leveraging their different experiences and networks in order to create change. Proper wisdom and accountability is necessary for EC planters to avoid the dangers of riches and to allow money and business to become a good steward instead of a bad master.

I would like to conclude this chapter with questions for church leaders and planters meant to stimulate further conversation and reflection. My hope is that churches will prioritize the identification and cultivation of the entrepreneurial mindset in their congregations in order to empower a new generation of wise EC planters.[39]

o   When and how does your church engage issues in the marketplace?

o   What messages are the laity hearing about their role in the marketplace to fulfill their missional calling (e.g., from biblical, theological, missiological, and historical sources, as well as contemporary examples)?

o   Who in your church exhibits an entrepreneurial mindset? Consider how they receive information and then act upon this information.

o   How could these entrepreneurs be engaged to form teams that reach the unchurched in the marketplace through ECP?

o   How can the church both encourage the right use of money and entrepreneurship without falling prey to the dangers of the same?

Abraham Kuyper famously claimed, "There is not a square inch in the whole domain of our human existence over which Christ, who is Sovereign over all, does not cry, Mine!"[40] EC planters attempt to live out this bold assertion by planting churches in the marketplace where Jesus says, "Mine!"

---

[1] Portions of the material for this chapter were originally published in W. Jay Moon, "Entrepreneurial Church Planting." *Great Commission Research Journal* 9.1 (2017): 56–70.

[2] Portions of this chapter were first published in W. Jay Moon, "Entrepreneurial Church Planting," *Great Commission Research Journal* 9.1 (2017): 56–70.

[3]   http://fortune.com/2017/04/21/steve-wozniak-apple-microsoft/

[4]   https://www.truity.com/blog/5-super-successful-introverts-and-what-they-did-right

[5] Heidi M. Neck, Christopher P. Neck, and Emma L. Murray, *Entrepreneurship: The Practice and Mindset* (Thousand Oaks, CA: Sage, 2018), 9.

[6] Ibid., 8.

[7] Ibid., 9.

[8] Ibid., 43.

[9] Ibid., 6.

[10] Ibid., 6.

[11] http://www.christianitytoday.com/edstetzer/2017/september/bivocational-ministry-as-evangelism-opportunity.html

[12] There are several resources available that summarize the characteristics of church planters including Winfield Bevins, *Church-Planting Revolution: A Guidebook for Explorers, Planters, and Their Teams* (Franklin, TN: Seedbed, 2017); Michael Moynagh and Philip Harrold, *Church for Every Context: An Introduction to Theology and Practice* (London: SCM, 2012); Stuart Murray, *Planting Churches in the 21st Century* (Scottdale, PA: Herald Press, 2010); Craig Ott and Gene Wilson, *Global Church Planting: Biblical Principles and Best Practices for Multiplication* (Grand Rapids: Baker Academic, 2011).

[13] Leslie Newbigin, *The Gospel in a Pluralist Society* (Grand Rapids: Eerdmans, 1989).

[14] To further read about examples of ECPs that arise from the Fresh Expressions movement in the UK, see https://freshexpressions.org.uk/

[15] To further read about examples of ECPs in South Korea, see the current research of Sang Rak Joo, *Entrepreneurial Church Planting (ECP) as a Model of Fresh Expressions in the South Korean context: Case Studies Exploring Relationships between Church Planting and Social Capital* (PhD dissertation at Asbury Theological Seminary, 2017) and Samuel Lee, "Faith in the Marketplace: Measuring the Impact of the Church in the Marketplace Through Entrepreneurial Church Planting" (PhD dissertation at Asbury Theological Seminary, scheduled for completion in 2018).

[16] E.g., Johnson Asare developed a hotel in a largely Muslim city, which also provides a venue for a church plant. See http://www.radach.org/site

[17] Consider the location of churches in shopping malls, such as in the Philippines. See http://www.dailymail.co.uk/wires/afp/article-

2914880/Eat-pray-shop-Philippines-embraces-mall-worshipping.html. Incidentally, malls in the U.S. that are finding it difficult to remain open are now opening up to churches as well. See https://www.wsj.com/articles/for-some-struggling-malls-churches-offer-second-life-1507633201

[18] This church planting approach appears to be on the rise in the U.S., according to the Fresh Expressions U.S. director. In addition to the cases presented in this chapter, see https://freshexpressionsus.org/

[19] Michael Goldsby, *The Entrepreneur's Tool Kit*, CD, The Great Courses (Chantilly, VA: The Teaching Company, 2014).

[20] For more information, see http://thecamphouse.com/

[21] http://mchatt.org/

[22] For more information on the church, see http://bluejeanselma.wixsite.com/bluejean

[23] Bob Armstrong, "A Proposal for The Millennial Project 2016" (Unpublished paper, 2016), 1.

[24] For further information, see Lee, Samuel, "A Sweet Fragrance: Networking and Partnership in Selma, AL" in *Social Entrepreneurship: Case Studies*, ed. W. Jay Moon, Roman Randall, and Joshua Moon (Nicholasville, KY: DOPS, 2017).

[25] Secular business writer Michael Goldsby chose this term "evangelist" to describe a particular type of entrepreneur that business people would recognize in the marketplace. Even though this term also has a biblical meaning, I chose to retain this term since it seems to provide a good bridge between the disciplines of entrepreneurship and church planting.

[26] http://meridzo.com/community-christian-center/

[27] Sentinel Group, *It's Only Cookie Dough*, DVD (Lynwood, WA, 2016).

[28] These tendencies were observed initially in my research on social entrepreneurs (some of whom are also the same EC planters described in the paradigm), and they are described further in: Robert Danielson, ed., *Social Entrepreneur: The Business of Changing the World* (Franklin, TN: Seedbed, 2015).

[29] Howard Dayton, *Business God's Way* (Orlando: Compass, 2014), 33.

30 As a church planter, co-owner in business, and full-time professor, I have experienced the difficulty of balancing all of these demands. I have relied upon a team of church planters (four) in our present church plant in order to help carry the load. It seems that ECP's especially highlight the need for church planting teams, like the Apostle Paul practiced, instead of the lone ranger "boot strapping" individual planting paradigm.

31 Eric Ries, *The Lean Startup: How Today's Entrepreneurs Use Continuous Innovation to Create Radically Successful Businesses* (New York: Crown Business, 2011).

32As quoted in Angela Eikenberry, "Refusing the Market: A Democratic Discourse for Voluntary and Non-Profit Organizations," *Nonprofit and Voluntary Sector Quarterly* 38.4 (2009): 582–96 at 584.

33 Luigino Bruni and Stefano Zamagni, *Civil Economy: Another Idea of the Market* (Newcastle upon Tyne, UK: Agenda, 2016), 17.

34 E.g., see Marc Benioff and Karen Southwick, *Compassionate Capitalism: How Corporations Can Make Doing Good an Integral Part of Doing Well* (Pompton Plains, NJ: Career, 2004).

35 Dorothy Sayers, *Creed or Chaos?: Why Christians Must Choose Either Dogma or Disaster (Or, Why It Really Does Matter What You Believe)* (New York: Harbcourt Brace, 1949), 56–57.

36 See Richard Higginson, "Mission and Entrepreneurship," *Anvil Journal of Theology and Mission* 33.1 (2017): 15–20. Higginson's recent research on kingdom businesses in the UK found that the Christian business owners identified the following means to express their kingdom impact: make the world a better place by providing an excellent product or service, embody Christian values in their workplace, share their faith in the marketplace, and giving to charitable and Christian causes.

37 https://www.umcmission.org/Find-Resources/John-Wesley-Sermons/Sermon-50-The-Use-of-Money

38 For developing a robust business model, I recommend that the following book is integrated with the Fresh Expressions model (shared in previous chapter) and implemented using Eric Ries' "Lean Startup" approach: Alexander Osterwalder and Yves Pigneur. *Business Model Generation: A Handbook for Visionaries, Game Changers, and Challengers* (Hoboken, NJ: John Wiley & Sons, 2010).

[39] See Greg Jones, *Christian Social Innovation: Renewing Wesleyan Witness* (Nashville: Abingdon, 2016). He stresses that Christian social innovation should be cultivated in churches through the emphasis on both tradition and innovation in what he calls "traditioned innovation."

[40] https://www.goodreads.com/author/quotes/385896. Abraham_Kuyper.

CHAPTER 9

Innovative Fresh Expressions of Church

Winfield Bevins

Introduction

In the spring of 2005, my wife and I moved to a small island in the Outer Banks of North Carolina in order to plant a new church. With nothing but a little faith, we began meeting in a home with only five people. Our vision for the church was simple, to be a local indigenous expression of the church for the Outer Banks. Thus, we named the church, Church of the Outer Banks. Over the next few years the church continued to grow and we witnessed dozens of people come to faith in Jesus Christ. Many of the church members were surfers who had little or no church background at all. As a result, the church began to intentionally engage the surfing community and over time we reached dozens of surfers for Christ. To engage the surfing community, I even learned how to surf and drove around with a surfboard strapped to the top of my car just in case there was a good wave!

The church was also involved in several marketplace outreaches to build bridges to the community in a number of creative ways. We adopted beach accesses, which the church cleaned once a month to show the community that the church cares about the beaches. The church began an art-mentoring program that has reached hundreds of at-risk youth in our community and reached kids as far away as South America. We eventually opened a non-profit art gallery that hosted art shows and concerts to build bridges between the church and community. In this creative space, the church hosted quarterly art shows that infused art, music, and coffee. These community art shows drew hundreds of people from the community. By embracing the community around us, our church was able to establish deep connections with the unchurched and continuously reach out to those around us in a meaningful way. What we didn't realize at the time was that by adopting this approach to ministry, we were a part of a larger movement of new ways of church planting called "Fresh Expressions."

Fresh Expressions of Church

So, what is a fresh expression? A fresh expression is "a form of church for our changing culture, established primarily for the benefit of people who are not yet members of any church."[1] The key points of emphases within this definition are the ideas of "changing culture" and reaching those not involved in existing churches. The Fresh Expressions movement began in England a little over a decade ago and has resulted in the birth of more than three thousand new communities alongside existing churches in the UK.[2] In 2003, the former Archbishop of Canterbury Rowan Williams called for an integration of church that would include both traditional and fresh expressions of church to meet the new challenges of a post-Christian and post-modern context. In his own words, "We have begun to recognize that there are many ways in which the reality of 'church' can exist.... These may be found particularly in the development of a mixed economy of Church life."[3]

The "mixed economy of church life" is an important concept since it describes how the church is to keep in tension two different ways of doing life or 'economies'—to support both the traditional (inherited) form of church and also the contemporary (contextual) forms of church. These new contextual "fresh expressions" often gather at venues away from the traditional church building but are still tethered to the traditional church in order to maintain unity. Detractors have argued that fresh expressions may lead to exclusivism and segregation according to the Homogeneous Unit Principle.[4] In reality, however, the mixed economy approach ultimately aims at the opposite: Groups that are already excluded from the church are sought out and reached by fresh expressions. As they gather in venues apart from the traditional church building, they are reconciled to God and ultimately the larger church.

The phrase "fresh expressions" comes from the preface to the Declaration of Assent, which Church of England ministers make at their ordination to affirm, "which faith the Church is called upon to proclaim afresh in each generation." The expression "fresh expressions" echoes these words and implies "something new or enlivened is happening, but also suggests connection to history and the developing story of God's work in the Church."[5] Within this larger framework, there are four tenets that describe what fresh expressions are:

o Missional—serving those outside church;
o Contextual—listening to people and entering their context;
o Educational—making discipleship a priority: journeying with people to Jesus;
o Ecclesial—forming church; they are not simply bridges to an existing church, but an expression of church for others in the midst of their lives.[6]

In 2004, the Church of England released the *Mission Shaped Church Report* that reflected on current fresh expressions and also made recommendations for the future practice of this pioneering mission. This report marked the beginning of the fresh expressions movement's path to becoming a global movement. The fresh expressions movement is beginning to take shape in other countries like South Korea, United States, Australia, Canada, and Germany[7]. Every fresh expression is different because, "there is no single model to copy but a wide variety of approaches for a wide variety of contexts and constituencies. The emphasis is on planting something which is appropriate to its context, rather than cloning something which works elsewhere."[8]

So, are fresh expressions actually making a difference? According to the Church of England's most recent research, they are. Between January 2012 and May 2016, over twenty-seven hundred cases from twenty-one dioceses were examined and the data came from interviewing key leaders. Commenting on the findings of the research, Phil Potter, the Archbishops' Missioner and Leader of Fresh Expressions said, "This is the most in-depth research we've had to date and it offers an encouraging and exciting snapshot of how the Church is finding fresh confidence in evangelism through fresh expressions."[9]

In addition to this report, the Church Army's Research Unit for the Church Commissioners carried out yet another detailed study in which Dr. George Lings, the Unit's Director, noted, "Nothing else in the Church of England has this level of missional impact and the effect of adding further ecclesial communities."[10] These studies have noted the explosions of this innovative movement. Below, I've listed just a few highlights of how the movement is impacting the UK.

- More than 50,600 people attend fresh expressions of church across half of the dioceses in the Church of England.
- The majority of those who attend are women, and younger than the average parish congregation.
- There are currently more than 3,400 reported fresh expressions congregations of all denominations across the UK.
- 40% of the people who are a part of fresh expressions have no significant church experience in their past, which demonstrates their missional nature.
- Some 44% of the fresh expressions in the research were launched between 2010 and 2012.
- A typical fresh expression begins with three to twelve people.
- An estimated 24.5% of those attending fresh expressions of church are already members of a church, 35.2% are people who used to belong to church but who left for one reason or another while 40.3% are those with no previous church background in all of the 13.5% of parishes in the dioceses surveyed that had started a fresh expression of church.
- 52% of the fresh expressions of church are led by people who are not ordained, which indicates their grass roots lay-led nature.
- There are at least twenty different recognizable types of fresh expressions of church and the average size is forty-four.
- Fresh expressions of church can be found in all traditions in the Church of England. The fresh expressions of church meet in all kinds of venues at various times, days of the week and geographical settings. The world of fresh expressions of church is described as one of "varied and smaller communities."
- 78% of fresh expressions intentionally encourage discipleship, not just attract attenders.
- The majority (66%) either continue to grow numerically or maintain the growth gained.[11]

It is important to note that a fresh expression is not a model, but a contextualized way of planting new faith communities. As Neil Cole reminds us, "The answers are not found in our models, methods, and manmade systems but in the truth of God's Word and in being filled with the Spirit of God."[12] Each fresh expression is called to be the church in its unique context and culture. In *Church for Every Context*, author and researcher Michael Moynagh praises this contextualized approach to church for being able to "seek to fit the culture of the people they serve."[13] With regard to the diversity, no one model is better than the other. Each one has the ability to be used by the Spirit as it adapts to fit a specific context.

Fresh expressions of church aren't just a good idea; they flow from the mission of God. God is a sending God who compels us to join in God's mission. In His own words, Jesus proclaims, "As You sent Me into the world, I also have sent them into the world" (John 17:18 NASB). According to missiologist Christopher Wright, "Mission belongs to our God. Mission is not ours; mission is God's…. It is not so much the case that God has a mission for his church in the world but that God has a church for his mission in the world. Mission was not made for the church; the church was made for mission—God's mission."[14] According to Eddie Gibbs, professor emeritus of church growth at Fuller Theological Seminary, fresh expressions are intended to manifest "The Five Marks of Mission."[15] The Five Marks of Mission are:

1. To proclaim the Good News of the Kingdom;
2. To teach, baptize and nurture new believers;
3. To respond to human need by loving service;
4. To transform unjust structures of society, to challenge violence of every kind and pursue peace and reconciliation; and
5. To strive to safeguard the integrity of creation, and sustain and renew the life of the earth.

Examples of Fresh Expressions

There are endless examples of fresh expressions, such as dinner churches, biker churches, cowboy churches, even surfer churches like the one we started in the Outer Banks, North Carolina. Fresh Expressions meet in coffee houses, local pubs, bowling alleys, funeral homes, YMCAs, schools, and even outdoors under a tree.¹⁶ Enacting the mission of God takes all kinds of expressions of church to reach all kinds of people. In essence, each fresh expression is a mosaic or tapestry that consists of many colors. Each fragment displays a different color, but in unison, these individual pieces portray a beautiful masterpiece. Likewise, today there are many different expressions of church that make up the body of Christ.

The following example paints a picture of how a Fresh Expression is formed. There were three Christian women who loved to cook and lived in a small village in England. They began to invite local unchurched teenagers from their community to learn how to cook and then eat what they'd made together. As they ate together, they talked about their lives and the women were able to share their Christian faith with the youth. The meals always started with prayers of thanksgiving and the teenagers were invited to add what they were thankful for as well. Over time, the teenagers began to embrace Christianity and eventually a new Christian community was born.¹⁷ We see from this story that the aim of a Fresh Expression isn't to provide a steppingstone into an existing church, but to form a new kind of church that steps out in its own right.¹⁸

Another example of a fresh expression reminds us that while fresh expressions of church may look radically different from more traditional expressions of the church, they thrive best when launched in partnership with an established church. Church planter Luke Edwards planted King Street Church as a new fresh expression of church out of Boone United Methodist Church in 2013. Boone UMC wanted to reach those on the margins of their community, so they commissioned the birth of King Street Church. "We felt like the church was called to do more than serve," Luke Edwards, Pastor of King Street Church, said. "We're called to welcome, include, and worship with everyone. We still excluded the marginalized from the body because we served them, but didn't welcome them."¹ When examining what model or approach they were going to take for the new church, they chose to follow the Fresh Expressions model as they've found that presenting the traditional gospel in new ways made it easier for those unfamiliar with church to become a faith community.

In the beginning, Luke approached a few people exploring the Christian faith, but who were not necessarily Christians. This group of five to six spent three months eating together during the course of one summer. Gradually, this group became a community that worshiped together and dialogued about faith and life. King Street Church was born. Now, that group meets weekly in what they call Sundays at the Saloon. On Sunday evenings, Christians and non-Christians alike gather to read a passage of Scripture, apply it to their lives, ingest it, and wash it down with a cold beer. King Street currently offers a variety of gatherings designed with a specific group of people in mind. These include a ministry to inmates in the Watauga County Jail, college students, the homeless and businesspersons, service projects, the Single Mom Squad, and Death Café, which encourages open, honest conversations about the process of death and dying.[19] King Street is a wonderful example how a new fresh expression can partner with an existing church.

Starting a Fresh Expression

While each fresh expression of church is uniquely different, they come into being through principles of careful listening, service, contextual mission, and making disciples. So how do they work and what is the process of starting a fresh expression? Fresh expressions often emerge prayerfully as portrayed in the following image.[20]

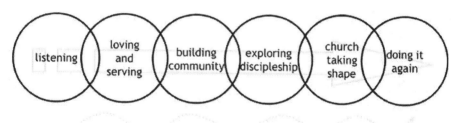

underpinned by prayer, ongoing listening and relationship with the wider church

Although each stage has its own value for the kingdom, there is a general pattern for starting a fresh expression.[21]

    1. <u>Listening</u>. Since contextualization and adaptation are at the heart of fresh expressions, those in leadership must begin with listening to God and listening to the people they are called to serve. Dr. Travis Collins, Director of Missional Advancement for Fresh Expressions US instructs, "Discernment of God's will is a key to fresh expressions of

church."[22] This involves discernment and prayer on behalf of the people who are starting a fresh expression of church. It is important to listen to God's voice and seek His direction in prayer when starting a fresh expression. He may speak through a still, small voice or through the needs and people within the community. This often involves participating in the life of the people and learning through research methods such as participant-observation, informal interviews, focus groups, etc. A lot of people see prayer as a monologue rather than a dialogue. However, to be faithful in starting a fresh expression, we can't simply talk to God; we must stop and receive what He is saying. Patience and the ability to listen are absolutely crucial.

2. Loving and Serving. Fresh expressions are birthed when leaders find a way to love and serve the people around them in a relatable manner. Michael Moynagh encourages that fresh expressions start with "serving first" instead of "worship first."[23] When starting a fresh expression, the core of the church needs to understand the needs of the people and find ways to serve others. This begins through canvasing the surrounding area, assessing the community, and getting to know neighbors and their families. Identifying key interests and communal connection points proves vital in this process.

3. Building Community. After gathering information about the surrounding context, the fresh expression can begin to take shape as the group of believers builds community with those they serve. The church is not a building but the family of God and the Body of Christ. Disciples are made through biblical, Christ-centered community. In the book of Acts, the life of the early church revolved around community. Acts 2:42 says, "They devoted themselves to the apostles' teaching and to fellowship, to the breaking of bread and to prayer" (NIV). Fresh expressions are deeply rooted in relationships and are built around community and fellowship.

4. Exploring Discipleship. Fresh expressions also invite people into deep connection with the church community by offering individuals chances to explore becoming disciples of Jesus. Fresh expressions can play an important role in the spiritual growth and development of others as disciples and followers of Jesus Christ. Graham Cray, Former Bishop of Maidstone in the Diocese of Canterbury and the Archbishops' Missioner and Team Leader of Fresh Expressions proclaims, "The long-term value of any expression of church, inherited or fresh, is to be judged by the sort of disciples it

makes."[24] While modern models may tend to value quantity, fresh expressions are not simply be concerned with growing numbers, but with growing people through discipleship. Fresh expressions allow people to ask important questions, dialogue, and learn from other believers who have more wisdom and experience.

     5. <u>Church Taking Shape</u>. Rather than importing a model, Fresh Expression lets a Christian community take shape around those coming to faith. This is a significant shift in thinking when it comes to church planting. Rather than starting with a predetermined model, fresh expressions actually grow from the bottom up instead of the top down. The Church of the Outer Banks is an example of how this happens. We started the church with only five people in a home and we didn't even have a name for the church, but as we began to reach people in the community, we learned from our interactions and adapted our church to the context. Through this process of dialogue between the church and the community, the church began to take shape and form its unique identity.

     6. <u>Doing it Again</u>. Fresh expressions encourage new believers to "do it again" by empowering those within the church community to lead others on a similar journey to start more fresh expressions. The goal is not to start a single fresh expression, but to start a movement that gives birth to multiple expressions throughout a city or community. In the words of Steve Addison, "It's not just about one new church. It's about a whole new generation of churches."[25] This movement begins with a vision to multiply communities through the leading of the Spirit. Its revolutionary perspective on church allows fresh expressions to continually give birth to new and exciting contextualized ways of being church for the twenty-first century.

Conclusion

Fresh expressions of church are an effective way of starting new contextualized faith communities that are working in a variety of contexts. Two things make fresh expressions especially effective for mission in the twenty-first century. First, they are often started with ordinary, non-ordained lay people. Because of the recognition of the power of the laity, fresh expressions offer a place for everyone to serve and get involved regardless of age, background, nationality, race, or gender. Statistically, fresh expressions have a higher involvement of lay people including women, children, families, the young, the elderly—fresh expressions are for everybody!

Second, fresh expressions of church don't have to be expensive and can meet in homes, coffeehouses, or other locations that do not require a lot of start-up money. They are often started with very little funding as opposed to traditional church planting models that require funding for clergy salaries and expensive buildings. In fact, many people are able to start a fresh expression of church on little to nothing. Many fresh expressions are finding unique ways to make disciples that do not require the expenses of traditional church buildings, structures, and staff salaries. Likewise, fresh expressions of church are an inexpensive alternative to expensive traditional models of church planting.

These final points highlight the strength of fresh expressions: They are empowered by the Spirit, formed through ordinary people, simply funded, and exist for the glory of God's kingdom. By listening to the context and holding on to the power of the Gospel at the same time, these new faith communities are able to speak with a powerful voice that influences people the traditional church may never reach. Fresh expressions of church are one way the Lord is using to reach people in a contextually meaningful way in the twenty-first century.

Many, but not all, fresh expressions are started in the marketplace as a means to connect people who would not otherwise come to church. The church planter can either start the fresh expression inside an existing business where people are already gathering or start a new business that would gather people. The latter option takes a bit more thought and planning, which is the topic of the next chapter.

---

¹ Travis Collins, *Fresh Expressions of Church* (Franklin, TN: Seedbed, 2015), 5.

² http://freshexpressions.org.uk/about/what-is-a-fresh-expression/

³ Archbishop's Council on Mission and Public Affairs, *Mission-Shaped Church: Church Planting and Fresh Expressions in a Changing Context* (New York: Seabury, 2009), 26.

⁴ See, e.g., Andrew Davison and Alison Milbank, *For the Parish: A Critique of Fresh Expressions* (London: SCM, 2010). These authors provide other critiques such as thin theology and ecclessiology (which were later addressed by others). They also note that forms cannot be too

easily disconnected from meanings. This latter critique has been addressed by various missiologists in order to promote contextualization in missional settings such as many present day Western cultures. For example, see W. Jay Moon, *Intercultural Discipleship: Learning from Global Approaches to Spiritual Formation.* Encountering Mission Series (Grand Rapids: Baker Academic, 2017).

[5] Ibid., 34.

[6] http://community.sharetheguide.org/guide/about/whatis

[7] http://community.sharetheguide.org/international

[8] See https://www.freshexpressions.org.uk/about/whatis

[9] http://community.sharetheguide.org/news/anglicanresearch

[10] http://community.sharetheguide.org/news/anglicanresearch

[11] For the full report see https://www.churcharmy.org.uk/Group/Group.aspx?id=286719

[12] See Neil Cole, *Organic Church: Growing Faith Where Life Happens* (San Francisco: Jossey-Bass, 2005).

[13] Michael Moynagh, *Church for Every Context: An Introduction to Theology and Practice* (London: SCM Press, 2012), 194.

[14] Christopher J. H. Wright, *The Mission of God: Unlocking the Bible's Grand Narrative* (Downers Grove, IL: InterVarsity, 2006), 62.

[15] Eddie Gibbs, *ChurchMorph: How Megatrends are Reshaping Christian Communities*, Allelon Missional Series (Grand Rapids: Baker Academic, 2009), 65. The Five Marks of Mission were developed at the sixth meeting of the Anglican Consultative Council in 1984.

[16] Various examples of the diversity of Fresh Expressions exist. In the UK, see http://freshexpressions.org.uk/; in the United States, see http://freshexpressionsus.org; and in Canada, see https://www.freshexpressions.ca.

[17] From https://www.freshexpressions.org.uk/guide/essential/whatare.

[18] See http://freshexpressionsus.org/about/what-is-a-fresh-expression

[19] For more information on Luke and King Street Church, visit http://asburyseminary.edu/voices/luke-edwards.

[20] The image is from http://community.sharetheguide.org/guide/develop/journey

²¹ I have drawn the following six points from the Fresh Expressions website http://community.sharetheguide.org/guide/essential/howtostart. See also Travis Collins, *Fresh Expressions of Church.*

²² Collins, *Fresh Expressions of Church*, 54.

²³ Moynagh, *Church for Every Context*, 205–10. While many church planters start their church by a big "launch day" through a worship service, fresh expressions often start by serving the community first and then the worship comes later.

²⁴ Archbishop's Council on Mission and Public Affairs, *Mission-Shaped Church*, ix.

²⁵ Steve Addision, *Movements that Change the World: Five Keys to Spreading the Gospel.* (Downers Grove, IL: IVP, 2011), 38.

CHAPTER 10

Starting Points:
Robust Missiology in the Marketplace

W. Jay Moon

Introduction

I have talked with numerous church planters who are eager to engage the marketplace and engage in the work of entrepreneurial church planting (ECP). I am encouraged and excited by the numerous examples of entrepreneurial church (EC) planters, both those described in the previous chapters and those who we simply did not have time to mention.[1] In this concluding chapter, I would like to suggest some possible starting points for those who would like to explore this option of church planting.

To make a robust EC plant requires both a robust missiology as well as a robust business model. In traditional church planting discussions, business men and women were not considered essential except to finance and support the mission. The unspoken message was that the real value of their business work was to use their profits to support the "spiritual work." While I applaud the generous use of profits from excellent work, my hope is that business people now find that they have a front seat at the church planting table. In short, your work matters to God![2] Even further, you will likely find the opportunity to live out your missional calling *within* the marketplace, not *in spite of* the marketplace.

When Jesus discussed the cost of being a disciple, he said,

> Suppose one of you wants to build a tower. Won't you first sit down and estimate the cost to see if you have enough money to complete it? For if you lay the foundation and are not able to finish it, everyone who sees it will ridicule you, saying, 'This person began to build and wasn't able to finish' (Luke 14:28-31).[3]

In order to "count the cost" from a business perspective, venture capitalist and entrepreneur Sam Altman from Stanford (who has funded 720 businesses) recommends that entrepreneurships consider four key ingredients:

1. Good idea (that solves a need and people will pay for),
2. Good product/service (something users love and will tell others about),
3. Good team (that are smart, get things done, and work together well), and
4. Good execution (deliver with excellence in the right metrics and milestones).[4]

Understanding and applying these key ingredients will help EC planters to wisely 'build the tower.' Thus, in this chapter, I will discuss the necessary foundational steps for ECP within the framework of entrepreneurship as described by Altman. The steps are described under the acronym ABIDES—Ask, Begin, Incubate, Develop, Excel, Sustain. The acronym reminds us that our ECP efforts depend integrally on abiding as branches in the Vine of the Lord who nourishes us (John 15). This approach will build upon the Fresh Expressions process described in the last chapter in order to lay a missiological foundation. Then, we will integrate this with the Business Model Canvas (to be discussed shortly) to plan out the business approach for the EC plant. Lastly, we will implement the EC plant using the Lean Startup approach with pivots in a quick feedback loop (also to be discussed shortly).

Ask the Lord for Discernment and Direction

Prayer is often the starting point for great endeavors. Jesus himself, when burdened with compassion for the lost people around him, asked his disciples to pray that the Lord of the Harvest would send out workers for the harvest (Matt 9:36–38). Then in the next verse at 10:1, Jesus prepared his disciples for ministry and sent them out. This pattern of observation, burden, prayer, and action appears to be a model of God prompting people for ministry. The Apostle Paul at Athens was moved in his spirit when seeing the idolatry and lostness around him. He must have been in constant prayer; and then he acted by witnessing in the synagogue and "in the market place every day with those who happened to be present" (Acts 17:17 NASB). Something similar is seen in the Apostle Paul's epistles that usually begin with thanksgiving and/or prayer; often these prayers contain seminal ideas that Paul develops in the rest of the letter (e.g., 1 Cor 1:4–9; 1 Thess 3:11–13). It is almost as if Paul's constant praying for people prepared him to write the letter about the very themes he was praying. This process of ECP likewise involves the prayerful preparation that leads to purposeful, missional endeavors. This prayer will be prompted in conjunction with careful observation of people and their needs (see below) and will involve both one's longing for something more and one's listening to the Lord. It is important to pay attention to the Spirit's prompting and the yearnings that spring up in the heart. Then, be prepared to move in mission.

Begin with a Good Idea

Altman affirms, "The best ideas are mission-oriented.... There is no way to get through the pain of a startup unless you believe that the startup really matters."[5] The Fresh Expression approach provides a helpful starting point for the business idea that is mission-oriented. The first step in Fresh Expressions is to listen to the community.

Listening often requires taking the time to engage people through ethnographic research methods. Participant-observation is a research method that allows the potential church planter to participate with the people long enough and deeply enough that the people express their true needs, desires, aspirations, and dreams. In addition to the needs, look for the assets that reside in this community. This provides an indication into their strengths that can be built upon as well as their pains that need to be addressed. Recording these participant-observations gives you research data during the listening process.

Researchers often use informants to give them deeper insight. Characteristics of good informants are those who ...

o   Know their context well (i.e., they are 'regulars' vs. newcomers),
o   Are currently involved in the context,
o   Are sociable and verbal,
o   Have time for you,
o   Are located nearby, and
o   Are not overly analytical (they just tell you what they know).

Informal interviews with informants involve a series of friendly conversations into which the interviewer slowly introduces new elements to assist the informant. In practice, this is really relationship building instead of simply interviewing. After a while, these informants may be grouped together with others into a focus group. A small focus group (six to twelve people) can represent the larger context and provide helpful responses to questions that you formulate based on the initial participant-observations. Gradually, this research should lead to a good idea for a business that expresses love through service.

Incubate a Good Product or Service

The next logical step in the Fresh Expressions approach is to find opportunities to love and serve the people that you have been listening to. As you start to love and serve in small ways, then God may present larger opportunities. This will incubate a good product or service that will serve as the basis for your business. Keep in mind that this must be based on a missional foundation. It should be a calling from God and not simply a profit-making venture. Often, EC planters have found good traction in the service businesses since that provides daily conversations with larger networks of people. Once you have discovered a good idea to form a good product/service that you feel expresses your love for God and others, the next step is to organize this into a business model.

Alexander Osterwalder and Yves Pigneur explain, "A business model describes the rationale of how an organization creates, delivers, and captures value."[6] They developed an approach called the Business

Model Canvas to provide "a practical guide for visionaries, game changers, and challengers eager to design or reinvent business models."[7] There are nine elements to this approach that serve as the building blocks for developing a business model. The nine elements are mapped out on paper to demonstrate the logical connections between them.[8] Sites such as www.strategyzer.com provide explanations of the nine elements as well as downloads to start the process of mapping out your business model with your church planting team.[9] The nine elements are as follow:

1. Value proposition = What needs can I solve for customers? This is what you developed from your research based upon the first two steps in the Fresh Expressions approach above.
2. Customer segments = Who will pay to solve this need and where are they located? Why would they buy this?
3. Channels = How do you distribute the products or provide the service to customers?
4. Customer Relationships = How do I get, keep, and grow customers? From a missional perspective, ask, "How can I continue to demonstrate love for others through serving them well?"
5. Revenue Streams = How does your business make money from each customer segment?
6. Key resources = What assets do you need to make this company work? Think of physical equipment, human resources, software, social networks, spiritual trust, etc.
7. Partners = Who are the key partners and suppliers, and what do you need them to perform and when?
8. Key Activities = What are most important activities that you need to perform to make this business work?
9. Cost Structure = What costs and expenses are expended to make this product or service? Consider fixed and variable costs, your breakeven point, and the Return on Investment.

These nine items do not ensure a viable and mission focused business but they do provide critical areas to consider to keep on track. As you begin to map out the Business Model Canvas, you will quickly realize that you do not have all of the skills or capacity for each of the items needed. That is why it is critical to develop a good team of people who have the necessary skills and gifts.

Develop a Good Team

I have not met an EC planter yet who did not admit their need for a team of skilled people to come alongside of them. You will need people skilled in accounting, finance, organizational planning, taxes, etc. If you do not recruit a team with these skills, then you will quickly find yourself over your head and on a quick road to burnout. This is a great opportunity to approach people in the church that have these skills and gifts so that you can invite them into the missional opportunity of ECP. Perhaps for the first time, these business people will be validated that they are essential to the *missio Dei*.

In addition to the business skills above, the EC planter will need to build a team that knows how to evangelize in word, deed, and lifestyle. While evangelism has become more complex in the 21st century than at the beginning of the 20th century, there are new opportunities for evangelism that did not exist in a previous generation as well. Dealing with issues like secularism, pluralism, individualism, relativism, identity-shifting, and technology are critical considerations for EC planters. Each of these complexities also provide opportunities for evangelism.[10]

Excel at Good Execution

Eric Ries observed that entrepreneurs often have three limitations that prevent them from initiating and executing their business.[11] As shown in Figure 1 below,[12] the three obstacles are:

1. Incomplete Business Plans: Few EC planters are experienced with articulating business plans that address the concerns that venture capitalists are looking for. Resources have been addressed to assist in this process but this can still be a daunting task.[13]
2. Untested Market Demands: One of the biggest uncertainties about your proposed business is "Will people buy this good or service?" Since you have not fully tried out your business yet, you do not have an adequate answer.
3. Inadequate funding: To launch a full business with all of the services that you would like to offer would require a lot of funding. In addition, some organizations recommend that you acquire $300,000 to $500,000 to last for the first three years of operation in a typical "attractional" church plant.[14] Finding

this amount of money is not easy, particularly when you consider that there is not guarantee the church plant will survive after burning through the entire amount after three years.

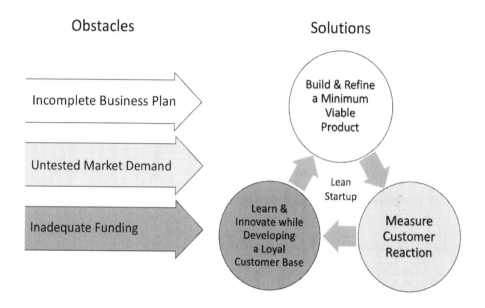

Figure 1—Startup Obstacles & Response with Lean Startup Approach

In order to overcome these obstacles, Ries recommends that you do not launch your business with all of the services and products exactly the way that you like. Instead, provide the minimum viable product (MVP) that would allow you to demonstrate what your business is offering. This means that you invest a small amount in order to get a product or service that people can experience. The initial value is **not** the amount of profit that you make; rather, Ries recommends that you initially measure your success by the amount of validated learning that you gain. In other words, allow customers to experience your business and then they provide feedback to tell you what they would prefer. The customer reaction then gives you valuable information to help you innovate and revise your business. At the same time, you are building a core group of customers that are teaching you what they want and they appreciate your responsiveness to adapt to

their needs. This develops a loyal base of customers and forms a
community. This is similar to the third step in the Fresh Expressions
approach about "building community." The last part of the feedback
loop is to take this information and revise/refine your MVP. Then,
send it back through the feedback look again.

This level of execution requires attentiveness and a quick
response to customers' needs and concerns. You will likely realize that
your service to these customers may be the very way that God has
provided for you to fulfill the Great Commandment, i.e., your business
is now demonstrating love to others by meeting their needs better and
demonstrating your love for God by using your God-given gifts and
abilities to serve others with excellence.[15]

Sustain by Introducing Metrics

For EC planters, the topic of metrics is very important. A well-known
maxim is, "What gets measured, gets done."[16] In other words, the
metrics that you pay attention to will affect how you direct your
energies. For all businesses, they must look at financial metrics. If there
is no profit, then the business will eventually close and it will not
provide a service to anyone. John Wesley wisely encouraged Christian
business owners to make as much profit as they can and save (not waste
profit) as much as they can. While these are necessary conditions for
business, they are not sufficient, though, for an ECP. In addition, ECP
planters must also use gauge their success via two other metrics: social
capital and spiritual capital.

Social capital can be measured in various ways. The point is
that this should be reported just as regularly as the financial capital
numbers are reported. For example, EC planters can measure:

1. Stories of lives that are being transformed,
2. Networks that the EC plant is connecting with (cf. Paul and the
   guilds),
3. How the health and welfare (physically and emotionally) of the
   workers and community are affected positively by the business.

In addition to social capital, EC planters should be measuring and
reporting spiritual capital. Church planters often measure this by
quantitative data like the number of conversions, baptisms, small

groups, etc. In addition to quantitative measures, EC planters can provide qualitative data, such as:

1. How the business has been generous in the community (cf. John Wesley's encouragement to give all that you can);
2. Signs of the Kingdom inside and around the EC plant;
3. Spiritual conversations that are started with the unchurched or de-churched;
4. Outward evidences of inward change, such as asking more and better questions about Jesus, baptism, prayer, etc.; and
5. Measures of accountability being used by the business team.

Paying attention to these metrics keeps the focus on exploring discipleship (Fresh Expressions step 4) instead of simply building a business that is focused on profit alone.

Conclusion

To offer a "conclusion" to this book seems like a misnomer. Instead of concluding the discussion and dreaming about ECP opportunities, I really feel like this is just the beginning. Here is my dream…

This may be the generation that is not satisfied with a Sunday only Christian experience that is separated from their everyday work life. This generation may finally wake up and say that their work actually matters to God. This generation may say that they are not content with abdicating their voice in the market square and simply relegating their voice to their private homes and worship buildings. This generation may not be content with a church building being vacant most of the week while it could be utilized for kingdom potential every day of the week. This generation may say that the secularization slide that is rampant in Europe is inevitable in North America. This generation may finally realize that most Christians will likely find that they can fulfill their missional calling in obedience to the *missio Dei **within*** the marketplace and then equip them to do so.

If this captures your thoughts and you are willing to explore ECP, then we welcome you to dream further. I hope that you will explore, act, learn, and respond to the need for church planting in the marketplace.

To encourage this process, Asbury Theological Seminary (ATS) has developed a Church Planting Institute that will come to your venue and provide six key modules for effective church planting. In addition, the Asbury Church Planting Fellows Program provides additional training and support, including some financial support, to a limited number of church planters.[17]

ATS's hope is that the theoretical foundations in this book provide sufficient biblical and theological support to encourage you to connect the dots in our generation for church planting in the marketplace. In addition, we hope that the practical examples gained from history up to this contemporary age will also inspire you to step out in faith to the God who calls us to be on mission.

I realize that this will ultimately be a work of the Holy Spirit. Like John Wesley, I think that our greatest days are still ahead of the church as we empower church planters, "… who fear nothing but sin and desire nothing but God, and I care not a straw whether they be clergymen or laymen, such alone will shake the gates of hell and set up the kingdom of heaven upon earth."[18]

This describes EC planters that innovate in the marketplace.

---

[1] The Fresh Expressions director in the U.S. mentioned that over 100 such churches have been planted across the U.S. in places like coffee shops, bars, cafes, workout facilities, pizza shops, etc. I wish there were time to mention more of these examples, such as The Table cafe started by United Methodist Pastor Larry Foss as an approach to plant an ECP in a marginalized section of Louisville, KY. See http://www.tablecafe.org/

[2] For a further elaboration of this from a pastoral perspective, see Tom Nelson, *Work Matters: Connecting Sunday Worship to Monday Work* (Wheaton, IL: Crossway, 2011).

[3] All Scripture quotations are from the NIV unless otherwise noted.

[4] https://www.youtube.com/watch?v=CBYhVcO4WgI

[5] Ibid.

[6] Alexander Osterwalder and Yves Pigneur, *Business Model Generation: A Handbook for Visionaries, Game Changers, and Challengers* (Hoboken, NJ: John Wiley & Sons, 2010), 14.

[7] Ibid, 5.

[8] For a quick demonstration, see https://www.youtube.com/watch?v=IP0cUBWTgpY.

[9] To download a copy of the business model canvas, as well as acccss additional resources for business startups, go to: https://strategyzer.com/canvas

[10] See the following video-enhanced i-Book to understand and address these concerns by W. Jay Moon, Timothy Robbins, Irene Kabete, eds. *Practical Evangelism for the 21st Century: Complexities and Opportunities* (Nicholasville, KY: DOPS, 2017).

[11] Eric Ries, *The Lean Startup: How Today's Entrepreneurs Use Continuous Innovation to Create Radically Successful Businesses* (New York: Crown Business, 2011).

[12] This graphic was developed by the graphic software company "Smartdraw" in an email correspondence to the author in 2017.

[13] Asbury Theological Seminary has developed the following resource to assist social entrepreneurs to develop their businesses, which can also assist ECP planters; see Robert A. Danielson, ed. *Social Entrepreneur: The Business of Changing the World* (Franklin, TN: Seedbed Publishing, 2015).

[14] This was the number quoted to potential church planters at the Exponential East church planting conference in the spring of 2017.

[15] Drawing from Matthew 25 and Martin Luther, this point is made by Gene Edward Veith, Jr., *God at Work: Your Christian Vocation in All of Life* (Wheaton, IL: Crossway, 2002).

[16] For further explanation about shifting church metrics to be more missional, see Reggie McNeal, *Missional Renaissance: Changing the Scorecard for the Church*, Jossey-Bass Leadership Network Series (San Francisco: Jossey Bass, 2009).

[17] To learn more, please visit https://asburychurchplanting.com/fellowship/

[18] John Wesley at 87 years old wrote this to Alexander Mather, quoted in Luke Tyerman, *The Life and Times of the Rev. John Wesley*, 2nd. ed. 3 vols. (London: Hodder and Stoughton, 1871), III:632.

WORKS CITED

CHAPTER 1

"Introducing Entrepreneurial Church Planting"

by W. Jay Moon

Armstrong, Bob. "A Proposal for The Millennial Project 2016." Unpublished, 2016.

Cooney, Thomas M. "Editorial: What Is an Entrepreneurial Team?" *International Small Business Journal* 23.3 (2005): 226–35.

Forster, Greg. "Introduction: What Are People Made For?" Pages 6–10 in *The Pastor's Guide to Fruitful Work and Economic Wisdom*, edited by Greg Forster and Drew Cleveland. Grand Rapids: Made to Flourish, 2012.

Goldsby, Michael. *The Entrepreneur's Tool Kit*. CD. The Great Courses. Chantilly, VA: The Teaching Company, 2014.

Hemphill, Ken, and Kenneth Priest. *Bonsai Theory of Church Growth*. Revised and Expanded edition. Tigerville, SC: Auxano, 2011.

Keener, Craig S. *The IVP Bible Background Commentary: New Testament*. 2nd ed. Downers Grove, IL: InterVarsity, 2014.

Kinghorn, Kenneth Cain. "Offer Them Christ with Bibles in Hand & God's Spirit in their Hears, the Early Circuit Riders," *The Asbury Herald* 117.1 (2007): 10–13.

Lee, Samuel. "Can We Measure the Success and Effectiveness of Entrepreneurial Church Planting?" *Evangelical Review of Theology* 40.4 (2016): 327–45.

Moon, W. Jay. "Entrepreneurial Church Planting." *Great Commission Research Journal* 9.1 (2017): 56–70.

Moynagh, Michael, and Philip Harrold. *Church for Every Context: An Introduction to Theology and Practice*. London: SCM, 2012.

Newbigin, Lesslie. *The Gospel in a Pluralist Society*. Grand Rapids: Eerdmans, 1989.

Sentinel Group. *It's Only Cookie Dough*. DVD. Lynwood, WA, 2016.

Stevens, R. Paul. *Work Matters: Lessons from Scripture*. Grand Rapids: Eerdmans, 2012.

Tennent, Timothy. "Homiletical Theology." Opening Convocation

Address, Asbury Theological Seminary, September 2016.
http://timothytennent.com/2016/09/13/my-2016-opening-convocation-address-homiletical-theology/.

Walls, A. F. *The Missionary Movement in Christian History: Studies in the Transmission of Faith*. Maryknoll, NY: Orbis, 1996.

Willard, Dallas, and Gary Black Jr. *The Divine Conspiracy Continued: Fulfilling God's Kingdom on Earth*. New York: Harper One, 2014.

Wright, David. *How God Makes the World A Better Place: A Wesleyan Primer on Faith, Work, and Economic Transformation*. Grand Rapids: Christian's Library Press, 2012.

CHAPTER 2

"Old Testament Foundations:
A Vision for a Holy Missional Community"

by Brian D. Russell

Allender, Dan B. *Sabbath*. Ancient Christian Practices. Nashville: Thomas Nelson, 2009.

Arnold, Bill T. *Genesis*. The New Cambridge Bible Commentary. Cambridge: Cambridge University Press, 2009.

Bauckham, Richard. *The Bible and Mission: Christian Witness in a Postmodern World*. Grand Rapids: Baker Academic, 2003.

Birch, Bruce C. *Let Justice Roll Down: The Old Testament, Ethics, and the Christian Life*. Louisville: Westminster John Knox, 1991.

Blackburn, W. Ross. *The God Who Makes Himself Known: The Missionary Heart of the Book of Exodus*. New Studies in Biblical Theology. Downers Grove, IL: IVP Academic, 2012.

Brueggemann, Walter. *Genesis*. Interpretation: A Bible Commentary for Teaching and Preaching. Louisville: John Knox, 1982.

Childs, Brevard S. *The Book of Exodus: A Critical, Theological Commentary*. OTL. Louisville: Westminster John Knox, 1974.

———. *Old Testament Theology in a Canonical Context*. Minneapolis: Fortress, 1985.

Currid, John D. *Against the Gods: The Polemical Theology of the Old Testament*. Wheaton, IL: Crossway, 2013.

Fretheim, Terence. *God and the World in the Old Testament: A Relational Theology of Creation.* Nashville: Abingdon, 2005.

Goheen, Michael. *A Light to the Nations: The Missional Church and the Biblical Story.* Grand Rapids: Baker Academic, 2011.

Hamilton, Victor P. *The Book of Genesis: Chapters 1–17.* New International Commentary on the Old Testament. Grand Rapids: Eerdmans, 1990.

Haydock, Nicholas. *The Theology of the Levitical Priesthood: Assisting God's People in Their Mission to the Nations.* Eugene, OR: Wipf and Stock, 2015.

Heschel, Abraham *The Sabbath.* Introduction by Susannah Heschel. FSG Classics. New York: Farrar Straus Giroux, 2005.

Janzen, Waldemar. *Exodus.* Believer's Church Bible Commentary. Harrisonburg, VA: Herald Press, 2000.

Janzen, Waldemar. *Old Testament Ethics: A Paradigmatic Approach.* Louisville: Westminster John Knox, 1994.

McBride, Jr., S. Dean. "Polity of the Covenant People: The Book of Deuteronomy." *Interpretation* 41.3 (1987): 229–44.

_____. "Yoke of the Kingdom: An Exposition of Deuteronomy 6:4–5." *Interpretation* 27.3 (1973): 273–304.

McKnight, Scott. *Jesus Creed: Loving God, Loving Others.* 10th Anniversary ed. Brewster, MA: Paraclete, 2014.

Middleton, J. Richard. *The Liberating Image: The Imago Dei of Genesis 1.* Grand Rapids: Brazos, 2005.

Moberly, R. W. L. *The Theology of the Book of Genesis.* Old Testament Theology. Cambridge: Cambridge University Press, 2009.

_____. *Old Testament Theology: Reading the Hebrew Bible as Christian Scripture.* Grand Rapids: Baker Academic, 2013.

Olson, Dennis. "The Jagged Cliffs of Mount Sinai: A Theological Reading of the Book of the Covenant (Exod 20:22–23:19)." *Interpretation* 50.3 (1996): 251–63.

Oswalt, John N. *Called to Be Holy.* Nappanee, IN: Evangel, 1999.

Russell, Brian D. *(re)Aligning with God: Reading Scripture for Church and World.* Eugene, OR: Cascade, 2015.

Sprinkle, Joe M. "Law and Narrative in Exodus 19–24." *JETS* 47.2 (2004): 235–52.

Wright, Christopher J. H. "Reading the Old Testament Missionally." Pages 107–23 in *Reading the Bible Missionally.* Ed. Michael W. Goheen. Grand Rapids: Eerdmans, 2016.

_____. *The Mission of God: Unlocking the Bible's Grand Narrative.* Downers Grove, IL: IVP Academic, 2006.

_____. *Old Testament Ethics for the People of God.* Downers Grove, IL: IVP Academic, 2011.

Wright, G. Ernest. *God Who Acts: Biblical Theology as Recital.* Studies in Biblical Theology 8. London: SCM, 1952.

CHAPTER 3

"The Business Behind and the Work Before Jesus"

by Fredrick J. Long

Awabdy, Mark A. and Fredrick J. Long. "Mark's Inclusion of 'For All Nations' in 11:17d and the International Vision of Isaiah." *The Journal of Inductive Biblical Studies* 1.2 (2014): 224–55 available at http://place.asburyseminary.edu/jibs/vol1/iss2/5/ and

Campbell, Ken M. "What Was Jesus' Occupation?" *Journal of the Evangelical Theological Society* 48 (2005): 501–19.

Cosden, Darrell. *A Theology of Work.* Eugene, OR: Wipf & Stock, 2006.

Drane, John William. *Introducing the New Testament.* Rev. ed. Oxford: Lion, 2000.

Eldred, Ken. *The Integrated Life.* Montrose, CO: Manna, 2010.

France, R. T. *The Gospel of Mark: A Commentary on the Greek Text.* New International Greek Testament Commentary. Grand Rapids: Eerdmans, 2002.

Gill, Theodore *Contributions to the Life Histories of Fishes.* Washington: Smithsonian Institution, 1909.

Goh, Benson. "The Charge of Being Deluded Interpreters of Scripture: A Reassessment of the Importance of Chiasms in Mark 11–12." *The Journal of Inductive Biblical Studies* 2.1 (2015): 30–61 available at http://place.asburyseminary.edu/jibs/vol2/iss1/4/.

Grudem, Wayne. *Business for the Glory of God.* Wheaton, IL: Crossway, 2003.

Holloman, Henry W. "Galilee, Galileans," *Baker Encyclopedia of the Bible.* Grand Rapids: Baker, 1988.

Issler, Klaus Dieter. *Living into the Life of Jesus: The Formation of Christian Character.* Downers Grove, IL: IVP, 2012.

Jensen, Morten Hørning. "Rural Galilee and Rapid Changes: An Investigation of the Socio-Economic Dynamics and Developments in Roman Galilee." *Biblica* 93.1 (2012): 43–67.

Liddell, Henry George, et al. *A Greek-English Lexicon*. Oxford: Clarendon, 1996.

Merk, August. "Magdala" in *The Catholic Encyclopedia*, Vol. 9. New York: Robert Appleton, 1910, available at http://www.newadvent.org/cathen/09523a.htm.

Meyers, Eric. "Jesus Probably Trilingual" transcript from *Jesus' Social Class* produced for Frontline at https://www.pbs.org/wgbh/pages/frontline/shows/religion/jesus/socialclass.html accessed 12-12-2017.

Moulton, James Hope and George Milligan. *The Vocabulary of the Greek Testament*. London: Hodder and Stoughton, 1930.

Novak, Michael. *Business as a Calling: Work and the Examined Life*. New York: Free Press, 1996.

Ryan, Jordan. "Tiberias" in *The Lexham Bible Dictionary*. Bellingham, WA: Lexham, 2016.

Schneider, John. *The Good of Affluence*. Grand Rapids: Eerdmans, 2002.

Tverberg, Lois. *Reading the Bible with Rabbi Jesus: How a Jewish Perspective can Transform your Understanding*. Grand Rapids: BakerBooks, 2017.

Whiston, William, translator. *The Works of Josephus: Complete and Unabridged*. Peabody, MA: Hendrickson, 1987.

Willard, Dallas. *"Some Steps Toward Soul Rest* in Eternal Living." Biola University Faculty Workshop, August 17, 2011.

Wong, Kenman and Scott Rae. *Business for the Common Good: A Christian Perspective for the Marketplace*. Downers Grove, IL: InterVarsity, 2011.

Zodhiates, Spiros. "Γαλιλαία" in *The Complete Word Study Dictionary: New Testament*. Chattanooga, TN: AMG, 2000.

CHAPTER 4

"Jesus's Entrepreneurial Teaching and His Earliest Disciples"

by Fredrick J. Long

Freyne, Sean. *Jesus, a Jewish Galilean: A New Reading of the Jesus Story*. London: T&T Clark, 2006.

Keener, Craig S. *The IVP Bible Background Commentary: New Testament*, 1st ed. Downers Grove, IL: InterVarsity, 1993.

Issler, Klaus Dieter. *Living into the Life of Jesus: The Formation of Christian Character*. Downers Grove, IL: IVP, 2012.

Long, Fredrick J. *Koine Greek Grammar: A Beginning-Intermediate Exegetical and Pragmatic Handbook*, Accessible Greek Resources and Online Studies. Wilmore, KY: GlossaHouse, 2015.

Longenecker, Bruce W. *Remember the Poor: Paul, Poverty, and the Greco-Roman World*. Grand Rapids: Eerdmans, 2010.

Longenecker, Bruce W. and Kelly D. Liebengood, eds., *Engaging Economics: New Testament Scenarios and Early Christian Reception*, 1st ed. Grand Rapids: Eerdmans, 2009.

Powell, Mark Allan. "Jesus and the Pathetic Wicked: Re-Visiting Sanders's View of Jesus' Friendship with Sinners." *Journal for the Study of the Historical Jesus* 13.2–3 (2015): 188–208.

Snodgrass, Klyne R. "Parable." Pages 591–601 in Joel B. Green and Scot McKnight, eds., *Dictionary of Jesus and the Gospels*. Downers Grove, IL: InterVarsity, 1992.

Wassell, Blake and Stephen Llewelyn. "'Fishers of Humans,' the Contemporary Theory of Metaphor, and Conceptual Blending Theory." *Journal of Biblical Literature* 133 (2014): 627–46.

Witherington III, Ben. *The Gospel of Mark: A Socio-Rhetorical Commentary*. Grand Rapids: Eerdmans, 2001.

CHAPTER 5

"Ecclesial Entrepreneurs in Acts and Paul"

by Fredrick J. Long

Alexander, Loveday. "Luke's Preface in the Context of Greek Preface-Writing." *Novum Testamentum* 28.1 (1986): 48–74.

Friberg, Barbara and Timothy. *Analytical Lexicon of the Greek New Testament*. Baker's Greek NT Library 4. Grand Rapids: Baker, 2000.

Goodrich, John K. "Managing God's Household: Overseers as Stewards and the Qualifications for Leadership in the Pastoral Epistles." Paper presented in the *Disputed Pauline Section* at the Society of Biblical Literature Annual Conference, San Francisco, November 21, 2011.

_____. "Overseers as Stewards and the Qualifications for Leadership in the Pastoral Epistles." *Zeitschrift für die Neutestamentliche Wissenschaft und Kunde der Älteren Kirche* 104 (2013): 77–97.

Halcomb, T. Michael W. *Paul the Change Agent: The Context, Aims, and Implications of an Apostolic Innovator*, GlossaHouse Dissertation Series 2. Wilmore, KY: GlossaHouse, 2015.

Hatch, Edwin. *The Organization of the Early Christian Churches. Eight Lectures Delivered Before the University of Oxford, in the Year 1880, on the Foundation of the Late Rev. John Bampton*. 3rd ed. London: Longmans, Green, and Co., 1918.

Hock, Ronald F. *Social Context of Paul's Ministry: Tent-Making and Apostleship*. Philadelphia: Augsburg Fortress, 1980.

Keener, Craig S. *Acts: An Exegetical Commentary*, 4 vols. Grand Rapids: Baker Academic, 2012.

Long, Fredrick J. *Ancient Rhetoric and Paul's Apology: The Compositional Unity of 2 Corinthians*, Society for the Study of the NT Monograph Series 131 (Cambridge: Cambridge University Press, 2004).

_____. "A Wife in Relation to a Husband: Greek Discourse Pragmatic and Cultural Evidence for Interpreting 1 Tim 2:11-15." *The Journal of Inductive Biblical Studies* 2.2 (2015): 6–43; available at http://place.asburyseminary.edu/jibs/vol2/iss2/3/.

Malherbe, Abraham J. "Overseers as Household Managers in the Pastoral Epistles." Pages 72–88 in *Text, Image, and Christians in the Graeco-Roman World a Festschrift in Honor of David Lee Balch*, ed. Aliou Cissé Niang and Carolyn A. Osiek. Princeton Theological Monograph Series 176. Eugene, OR: Pickwick, 2012.

Marshall, Peter. *Enmity in Corinth: Social Conventions in Paul's Relations with the Corinthians*. Wissenschaftliche Untersuchungen zum Neuen Testament 2.23. Tübingen: Mohr Siebeck, 1987.

Pollard, Edward B. "Commerce." *The International Standard Bible Encyclopaedia* ed. James Orr et al. Chicago: The Howard-Severance Company, 1915.

Robbins, Vernon K. "The Claims of the Prologues and Greco-Roman Rhetoric: The Prefaces to Luke and Acts in Light of Greco-Roman Rhetorical Strategies." Pages 63–83 in *Jesus and the Heritage of Israel: Luke's Narrative Claim Upon Israel's Legacy*, ed. David P. Moessner. Harrisburg, PA: Trinity Press International, 1999.

Winter, Bruce W. "The Entries and Ethics of Orators and Paul (1 Thessalonians 2:1–12)." *Tyndale Bulletin* 44.1 (1993): 55–74.

CHAPTER 6

"Great Commission: Theological Foundations
and Implications for Marketplace Ministry"

by Timothy C. Tennent

Beale, G. K. *The Temple and the Church's Mission.* Downers Grove, IL:
    InterVarsity Press, 2004.

Bosch, David. *Transforming Mission: Paradigm Shifts in Theology of Mission.*
    Maryknoll, NY: Orbis, 1991.

Carson, D. A. "The Purpose of the Fourth Gospel: John 20:31 Recon-
    sidered," *Journal of Biblical Literature* 106.4 (1987): 639–51.

Davis, Jack. "Teaching Them to Observe All that I Have Commanded
    You: The History of the Interpretation of the 'Great Commis-
    sion' and Implications for Marketplace Ministries." *Evangelical
    Review of Theology* 25 (2001): 65–80.

LaGrand, James. *The Earliest Christian Mission to 'All Nations' in the Light of
    Matthew's Gospel.* Atlanta: Scholars Press, 1995.

Larkin, William J., Jr. "Mission in Luke." Pages 152–69 in *Mission in the
    New Testament: An Evangelical Approach,* edited by William J. Lar-
    kin Jr. and Joel F. Williams. Maryknoll, NY: Orbis, 1998.

Marshall, I. Howard. *The Gospel of Luke,* NIGTC. Grand Rapids:
    Eerdmans, 1978.

McPolin, James, S. J., "Mission in the Fourth Gospel." *Irish Theological
    Quarterly* 36 (1969): 113–22.

Stock, Eugene. *History of the Church Missionary Society: Its Environment, Its
    Men, and Its Work.* Vol. 1. London: Christian Missionary Socie-
    ty, 1899.

Walls, Andrew. *The Missionary Movement in Christian History: Studies in the
    Transmission of Faith.* Maryknoll, NY: Orbis, 1996.

Wenham, John. *Easter Enigma: Are the Resurrection Accounts in Conflict?* Eu-
    gene, OR: Wipf and Stock, 2005.

Wishard, Luther. *A New Programme of Missions.* New York: Fleming H.
    Revell, 1895.

Wright, Christopher J. H. *The Mission of God: Unlocking the Bible's Grand
    Narrative.* Downers Grove, IL: IVP Academic, 2006.

CHAPTER 7

"Historical Perspective on Entrepreneurial Church Planting"
by Samuel Lee

Aprem, Mar. *Nestorian Missions*. Golden Jubilee Publications: No. 2. Trichur, Kerala: Mar Narsai Press, 1976.

Arntzen, A. M. *The Apostle of Norway: Hans Nielsen Hauge*. Eugene, OR: Wipf & Stock, 1933.

Bainton, Roland H. *Here I Stand: a Life of Martin Luther*. Reprint ed. Peabody: Abingdon, 1990.

_____. *The Reformation of the Sixteenth Century*. Enl. ed. Boston: Beacon, 1952.

Ballor, Jordan J. *Ecumenical Babel: Confusing Economic Ideology and the Church's Social Witness*. Grand Rapids: Christian's Library, 2010.

Banchoff, Thomas, and José Casanova, eds. *The Jesuits and Globalization: Historical Legacies and Contemporary Challenges*. Washington: Georgetown University Press, 2016.

Bevans, Stephen B., and Roger P. Schroeder. *Constants in Context: a Theology of Mission for Today*. Maryknoll, NY: Orbis, 2004.

Bosch, David Jacobus. *Transforming Mission: Paradigm Shifts in Theology of Mission*. Maryknoll, NY: Orbis, 1991.

Bruce, F. F. *The Spreading Flame: the Rise and Progress of Christianity from Its First Beginnings to the Conversion of the English*. Grand Rapids: Eerdmans, 1980.

Business as Mission Think Tank Group. *Business as Mission and Church Planting Fruitful Practices for Establishing Faith Communities*. BAM Think Tank, 2013. http://bamglobal.org/wp-content/uploads/2015/12/BMTT-IG-BAM-and-CP-Final-Report-January-2014.pdf (accessed November 27, 2017).

Danker, William J. *Profit for the Lord: Economic Activities in Moravian Missions and the Basel Mission Trading Company*. Grand Rapids: Wipf & Stock, 1971.

Eijnatten, Joris van, and Paula Yates. *The Churches. The Dynamics of Religious Reform in Church, State and Society in Northern Europe, 1780-1920: 2*. Leuven: Leuven University Press, 2010.

Forster, Greg. *Joy for the World: How Christianity Lost Its Cultural Influence and Can Begin Rebuilding It*. Wheaton, IL: Crossway, 2014.

Gallagher, Robert L., and John Mark Terry. *Encountering the History of Missions: from the Early Church to Today (Encountering Mission).* Grand Rapids: Baker Academic, 2017.

Herbert Spaugh, "A Short Introduction to the History, Customs, and Practices of the Moravian Church," http://newphilly.org/pdf/moravian.ashorthistory.pdf (accessed November 02, 2017).

Hunter, George G. *The Celtic Way of Evangelism: How Christianity Can Reach the West—Again.* 10th ed. Nashville: Abingdon, 2010.

Irvin, Dale T. and Scott Sunquist. *History of the World Christian Movement.* Maryknoll, NY: Orbis, 2001.

——————. *History of the World Christian Movement. Vol. 2, Modern Christianity from 1454-1800.* New York: Orbis, 2012.

Keplinger, Ksenia, Birgit Feldbauer-Durstmuller, Simon Sandberger, and Maximilian Neulinger. "Entrepreneurial Activities of Benedictine Monasteries—A Special Form of Family Business?" *International Journal of Entrepreneurial Venturing* 8.4 (January 1, 2016): 317.

Kim, Sangkeun. *Strange Names of God: the Missionary Translation of the Divine Name and the Chinese Responses to Matteo Ricci's.* New York: Peter Lang, 2005.

Ksenia Keplinger et al., "Entrepreneurial Activities of Benedictine Monasteries - a Special Form of Family Business?," *International Journal of Entrepreneurial Venturing* 8.4 (January 1, 2016): 317-333.

Lausanne Committee for World Evangelization. "Business as Mission: Lausanne Occasional Paper No. 59." Produced by the Issue Group on this topic at the 2004 Forum for World Evangelization, Pattaya, Thailand, September 29 to October 5, 2004.

Latourette, Kenneth Scott. *A History of the Expansion of Christianity, Vol 3, Three Centuries of Advance.* New York: Harper & Brothers, 1937.

Lee, Samuel. "Can We Measure the Success and Effectiveness of Entrepreneurial Church Planting?" *Evangelical Review of Theology* 40.4 (October 2016): 327–45.

Lim, David S. "Norway: The Best Model of a Transformed Nation Today." Davidlim53's Blog. https://davidlim53.wordpress.com/2011/09/02/norway-the-best-model-of-a-transformed-nation-today/ (accessed November 27, 2017).

Lowery, James L. *Case Histories of Tentmakers*, Wilton, CT: Morehouse-Barlow, 1976.

Moffett, Samuel Hugh. *A History of Christianity in Asia.* 2nd ed. Maryknoll, NY: Orbis, 1998.

Neill, Stephen, and Owen Chadwick. *A History of Christian Missions. The Penguin History of the Church: V. 6.* New York: Penguin Books, 1990.

Pachuau, Lalsangkima. "Missiology in a Pluralistic World: The Place of Mission Study in Theological Education." *International Review of Mission* 89.355 (October 1, 2000): 539–55.

Pocock, Michael, Gailyn Van Rheenen, and Douglas McConnell. *The Changing Face of World Missions: Engaging Contemporary Issues and Trends.* Grand Rapids: Baker Academic, 2005.

R.W. Hiebl Martin and Feldbauer-Durstmüller Birgit, "What Can the Corporate World Learn from the Cellarer?: Examining the Role of a Benedictine Abbey's CFO," *Society and Business Review* 1 (2014): 51–73.

Ramachandra, Vinoth. *The Recovery of Mission: Beyond the Pluralist Paradigm.* Grand Rapids: Eerdmans, 1997.

Saxby, Trevor. "Revival-Bringer: Hans Nielsen Hauge's Reformation of Norway." Making History Now. https://makinghistorynow.wordpress.com/2017/04/11/the-country-boy-who-fathered-a-nation-part-1/ (accessed November 02, 2017).

Scherer, James A. *Gospel, Church & Kingdom: Comparative Studies in World Mission Theology.* Eugene, OR: Wipf & Stock, 2004.

Sherman, Doug, and William D. Hendricks. *Your Work Matters to God.* Colorado Springs: NavPress, 1990.

Skeie, Karina Hestad. *Building Gods Kingdom: Norwegian Missionaries in Highland Madagascar 1866–1903.* Studies in Christian Mission. Leiden: Brill, 2012.

Smither, Edward L. *Mission in the Early Church: Themes and Reflections.* Cambridge: Cascade, 2014.

Snodderly, Ralph Winter and Beth. *Foundations of the World Christian Movement: a Larger Perspective Course Reader.* Pasadena, CA: Institute of International Studies, 2008.

Steffen, Tom A., and Mike Barnett, eds. *Business as Mission: from Impoverished to Empowered.* Edited by Tom A. Steffen and Mike Barnett. Pasadena, CA: William Carey Library, 2006.

Stevens, R. Paul. *The Other Six Days: Vocation, Work, and Ministry in Biblical Perspective.* Grand Rapids: Eerdmans, 1999.

Taylor, Mark C. *After God (Religion and Postmodernism)*. Chicago: University of Chicago Press, 2009.

Tillmanns, Walter G. "The Lotthers: Forgotten Printers of the Reformation." *Concordia Theological Monthly* 22.4 (April 1951): 260–64.

Tunehag, M., McGee, W. & Plummer, J. "Business as Mission. Lausanne Occasional Paper #59," 2004. Available at: http://www.lausanne.org/documents/2004forum/LOP59_IG30.pdf.

Veith, Gene Edward. Working for Our Neighbor: a Lutheran Primer On Vocation, Economics, and Ordinary Life. Grand Rapids: Christian's Library, 2016.

Villagomez, Cynthia Jan. "The Fields, Flocks, and Finances of Monks: Economic Life at Nestorian Monasteries, 500-850." Ph.D., University of California, Los Angeles, 1998.

Walter G Tillmanns, "The Lotthers: Forgotten Printers of the Reformation," *Concordia Theological Monthly* 22.4 (April 1951): 260-264.

Wee, Mons. O. *Haugeanism: A Brief Sketch of the Movement and Some of Its Chief Exponents,* St. Paul, MN: The Author, 1919.

Wesley, John, and Joseph Benson. *The Works of the Rev. John Wesley, Volume 10*. New York: J. & J. Harper, 1827.

Wesley, John. *The Works of the Reverend John Wesley, A.m.: Volume V*. Oxford: J. Emory and B. Waugh, 1833.

White, Charles Edward. "Four Lessons on Money from One of the World's Richest Preachers." *Christian History* 7/3.19 (January 1, 1988): 21–24.

Winter, Ralph D., and Steven C. Hawthorne, eds. *Perspectives On the World Christian Movement: A Reader (Perspectives)*. Edited by Ralph D. Winter and Steven C. Hawthorne. Pasadena, CA: William Carey Library, 2009.

Witherington, Ben. *Work: A Kingdom Perspective On Labor*. Grand Rapids: Eerdmans, 2011.

World History. "History of Monasticism." http://www.historyworld.net/wrldhis/PlainTextHistories.asp?gtrack=pthc&ParagraphID=eje#eje (accessed November 27, 2017).

Wright, David. *How God Makes the World a Better Place: A Wesleyan Primer on Faith, Work, and Economic Transformation*. Grand Rapids: Christian's Library Press, 2012.

CHAPTER 8

"Characteristics of Entrepreneurial Church Planters"

by W. Jay Moon

Armstrong, Bob. "A Proposal for The Millennial Project 2016" (Unpublished paper, 2016).

Benioff, Marc and Karen Southwick. *Compassionate Capitalism: How Corporations Can Make Doing Good an Integral Part of Doing Well* (Pompton Plains, NJ: Career, 2004).

Bevins, Winfield. *Church-Planting Revolution: A Guidebook for Explorers, Planters, and Their Teams* (Franklin, TN: Seedbed, 2017).

Bruni, Luigino and Stefano Zamagni, *Civil Economy: Another Idea of the Market* (Newcastle upon Tyne, UK: Agenda, 2016).

Danielson, Robert, ed. *Social Entrepreneur: The Business of Changing the World* (Franklin, TN: Seedbed, 2015).

Dayton, Howard. *Business God's Way* (Orlando, FL: Compass, 2014).

Eikenberry, Angela. "Refusing the Market: A Democratic Discourse for Voluntary and Non-Profit Organizations," *Nonprofit and Voluntary Sector Quarterly* 38.4 (2009): 582–96 at 584.

Goldsby, Michael. *The Entrepreneur's Tool Kit*, CD, The Great Courses (Chantilly, VA: The Teaching Company, 2014).

Higginson, Richard. "Mission and Entrepreneurship," *Anvil Journal of Theology and Mission* 33.1 (2017): 15–20.

Jones, Greg. *Christian Social Innovation: Renewing Wesleyan Witness* (Nashville: Abingdon, 2016).

Joo, Sang Rak. *Entrepreneurial Church Planting (ECP) as a Model of Fresh Expressions in the South Korean context: Case Studies Exploring Relationships between Church Planting and Social Capital* (PhD dissertation at Asbury Theological Seminary, 2017)

Lee, Samuel. "A Sweet Fragrance: Networking and Partnership in Selma, AL" in *Social Entrepreneurship: Case Studies*, ed. W. Jay Moon, Roman Randall, and Joshua Moon (Nicholasville, KY: DOPS, 2017).

Lee, Samuel. "Faith in the Marketplace: Measuring the Impact of the Church in the Marketplace Through Entrepreneurial Church Planting" (PhD dissertation at Asbury Theological Seminary, scheduled for completion in 2018).

Moon, W. Jay. "Entrepreneurial Church Planting." *Great Commission Research Journal* 9.1 (2017): 56–70.

Moynagh, Michael and Philip Harrold. *Church for Every Context: An Introduction to Theology and Practice* (London: SCM, 2012).

Murray, Stuart. *Planting Churches in the 21st Century* (Scottdale, PA: Herald Press, 2010);

Neck, Heidi M., Christopher P. Neck, and Emma L. Murray. *Entrepreneurship: The Practice and Mindset*. Thousand Oaks, CA: Sage, 2018.

Newbigin, Leslie. *The Gospel in a Pluralist Society* (Grand Rapids: Eerdmans, 1989).

Osterwalder, Alexander and Yves Pigneur. *Business Model Generation: A Handbook for Visionaries, Game Changers, and Challengers* (Hoboken, NJ: John Wiley & Sons, 2010).

Ott, Craig and Gene Wilson. *Global Church Planting: Biblical Principles and Best Practices for Multiplication* (Grand Rapids: Baker Academic, 2011).

Ries, Eric. *The Lean Startup: How Today's Entrepreneurs Use Continuous Innovation to Create Radically Successful Businesses* (New York: Crown Business, 2011).

Sayers, Dorothy. *Creed or Chaos?: Why Christians Must Choose Either Dogma or Disaster (Or, Why It Really Does Matter What You Believe)* (New York: Harbcourt Brace, 1949).

Sentinel Group, *It's Only Cookie Dough*, DVD (Lynwood, WA, 2016).

WEBSITES CITED:

Kuyper, Abraham. https://www.goodreads.com/author/quotes/385896.Abraham_Kuyper.

Asare, Johnson. http://www.radach.org/site

Blue Jean church in AL. http://bluejeanselma.wixsite.com/bluejean

Camp House in TN. http://thecamphouse.com/; http://mchatt.org/

Fresh Expressions in U.K. https://freshexpressions.org.uk/

Fresh Expressions in U.S. https://freshexpressionsus.org/

Introverted Entrepreneurs discussed. https://www.truity.com/blog/5-super-successful-introverts-and-what-they-did-right

Wesley, John (sermon). https://www.umcmission.org/Find-Resources/John-Wesley-Sermons/Sermon-50-The-Use-of-Money

Meridzo Ministry in KY. http://meridzo.com/community-christian-center/

Shopping mall churches. http://www.dailymail.co.uk/wires/afp/article-2914880/Eat-pray-shop-Philippines-embraces-mall-worshipping.html.

Shopping malls in U.S. https://www.wsj.com/articles/for-some-struggling-malls-churches-offer-second-life-1507633201

Stetzer, Ed. http://www.christianitytoday.com/edstetzer/2017/september/bivocational-ministry-as-evangelism-opportunity.html

Wozniak, Steve (about). http://fortune.com/2017/04/21/steve-wozniak-apple-microsoft/

CHAPTER 9

"Innovative Fresh Expressions of Church"

by Winfield Bevins

Addision, Steve. *Movements that Change the World: Five Keys to Spreading the Gospel.* Downers Grove, IL: IVP, 2011.

Archbishop's Council on Mission and Public Affairs. *Mission-Shaped Church: Church Planting and Fresh Expressions in a Changing Context.* New York: Seabury, 2009.

Cole, Neil. *Organic Church: Growing Faith Where Life Happens.* San Francisco: Jossey-Bass, 2005.

Collins, Travis. *Fresh Expressions of Church.* Franklin, TN: Seedbed, 2015.

Davison, Andrew and Alison Milbank. *For the Parish: A Critique of Fresh Expressions.* London: SCM, 2010.

Eddie, Gibbs. *ChurchMorph: How Megatrends are Reshaping Christian Communities.* Allelon Missional Series. Grand Rapids: Baker Academic, 2009.

Moon, W. Jay. *Intercultural Discipleship: Learning from Global Approaches to Spiritual Formation.* Encountering Mission Series. Grand Rapids: Baker Academic, 2017.

Moynagh, Michael. *Church for Every Context: An Introduction to Theology and Practice.* London: SCM Press, 2012.

Wright, Christopher J. H. *The Mission of God: Unlocking the Bible's Grand Narrative.* Downers Grove, IL: InterVarsity, 2006.

WEBSITES CITED:
Canadian fresh expressions: https://www.freshexpressions.ca.
How to Start a fresh expression:
        http://community.sharetheguide.org/guide/essential/howtostart.
International fresh expressions:
        http://community.sharetheguide.org/international
King St. Church: http://asburyseminary.edu/voices/luke-edwards.
Research on Anglican fresh expressions:
        http://community.sharetheguide.org/news/anglicanresearch
        https://www.churcharmy.org.uk/Group/Group.aspx?id=286719
U.K. fresh expressions:
        https://www.freshexpressions.org.uk/about/whatis
U.S. fresh expressions: http://freshexpressionsus.org
What is a fresh expression?
        http://freshexpressions.org.uk/about/what-is-a-fresh-
        expression;
        http://community.sharetheguide.org/guide/about/whatis

CHAPTER 10

"Starting Points: Robust Missiology in the Marketplace"

by W. Jay Moon

Danielson, Robert A., ed. *Social Entrepreneur: The Business of Changing the World*. Franklin, TN: Seedbed Publishing, 2015.
McNeal, Reggie. *Missional Renaissance: Changing the Scorecard for the Church*. Jossey-Bass Leadership Network Series. San Francisco, CA: Jossey Bass, 2009.
Moon, W. Jay, Timothy Robbins, Irene Kabete, eds. *Practical Evangelism for the 21st Century: Complexities and Opportunities*. Nicholasville, KY: DOPS, 2017.
Nelson, Tom. *Work Matters: Connecting Sunday Worship to Monday Work*. Wheaton, IL: Crossway, 2011.
Osterwalder, Alexander, and Yves Pigneur. *Business Model Generation: A Handbook for Visionaries, Game Changers, and Challengers*. Hoboken, NJ: John Wiley & Sons, 2010.
Ries, Eric. *The Lean Startup: How Today's Entrepreneurs Use Continuous Innovation to Create Radically Successful Businesses*. New York: Crown Business, 2011.

Tyerman, Luke. *The Life and Times of the Rev. John Wesley*. 2nd ed. 3 Vols. London: Hodder and Stoughton, 1871.

Veith, Jr., Gene Edward. *God at Work: Your Christian Vocation in All of Life*. Wheaton, IL: Crossway, 2002.

WEBSITES CITED:

Altman, Sam (on Entrepreneurship):
    https://www.youtube.com/watch?v=CBYhVcO4WgI

Asbury Theological Seminary (on Church Planting):
    https://asburychurchplanting.com/fellowship/

Business Model Canvas:
    https://www.youtube.com/watch?v=IP0cUBWTgpY

Business Model Assistance: www.strategyzer.com

Table Café: http://www.tablecafe.org/

For Notes

For Notes